Soft Tales
AND
HARD ASSES

ONE SALESMAN'S DISCOVERY OF
THE ART OF STORY TELLING

PAUL LANIGAN

ISBN: 1483979296
ISBN-13: 9781483979298

Library of Congress Control Number: 2013906492
CreateSpace Independent Publishing Platform
North Charleston, South Carolina

WHY STORIES?

Stories engage and intrigue but what is their role? Is it entertainment, education or are they a tool?

If sales is your bread and butter, take a hint. It pays to warm the butter before you spread it.

In 1979 there was a great deal of excitement in my hometown, as we were selected to host a pro-am golf tournament. It must be said that in the Ireland of the 1970s, there was a glamour and exclusivity about golf, which tended to be played by well-heeled folk driving fancy cars up long drives to exclusive clubs. Despite this, most lay people still had a broad understanding and appreciation of what the game involved, thanks to the exploits of Ireland's two pioneering golf heroes, Christy O'Connor Sr. and Christy O'Connor Jr.

My own exposure to the game was confined to what appeared alongside the football-league tables on the back of the Sunday newspaper. Given the fact that I usually found myself trying to read of my team's progress while an adult was reading the other side of the paper, I didn't have much opportunity to delve too deeply into the careers of the two Christy O'Connors.

One man who knew a links from a green and putter from a five iron was my math teacher Mr. Murphy, otherwise known as "Spud"—though not to his face, you understand. In fact, it's safe to say he was an avid golf fan and visibly excited by the prospect of having golf aristocracy grace our humble locality. You can imagine his preoccupation, as the usual classroom math metaphors of apples and oranges were increasingly replaced by more sport-oriented fare: "If Christy has five balls and Arnold has ten..." You get the picture.

In the week preceding the pro-am tournament, Spud was, as we say in Ireland, "up to ninety." Much to his delight, he had been given a role to play in the sacred event. I remember being impressed by this at the time, but in adult hindsight, I realize that the organizers had probably given him a task to get him out from under their feet. Spud's task was to recruit caddies to serve the gods of golf as they graced our humble turf with their footprints. He appeared in class one morning with a smile stretching from earlobe to earlobe—, a smile that told each and every one of us that rumors of a surprise test were unfounded. Instead, he announced that he was looking for volunteers to serve these sporting giants. In addition to the extraordinary honor of sharing airspace with the pantheon of greats, we would also be paid.

I don't know whether it was the pay, the privilege, the desire to be picked for something, or the prospect of time off from school, but my hand shot up at a speed Spud would not have had a formula to calculate. My enthusiasm—seen by Spud as representative of my love for the game—was noted, and straightaway I was picked.

By the following Thursday, my enthusiasm, still unabated, was now accompanied by the sort of youthful confidence that had me believing in my own fantasies: I was going to be on television; I was going to be spotted by the leading pro and recruited as his regular, favored caddie; girls were going to recognize me. I'm sure I anticipated writing about my experience in my memoirs. As I approached the as yet unopened gate of the golf club, I was mentally spending the few pounds I had yet to earn on a variety of teenage must-haves—clothing, music, and sport-related items, naturally.

I had arrived before the groundsmen and had to wait a good hour before the group of men (they were, in fact, all men) wearing funny clothes exited the dressing room and filed out onto the grass. I walked out of the clubhouse, determined to look the part by mimicking the casual but purposeful amble of the men who preceded me. It was at this point that I realized what had inspired Spud's awe. In the hour I had been waiting in the clubhouse, the grounds had filled with literally thousands of people, who stood as close as they could to the tape designed to distinguish the area of play from the spectator area.

I spotted a lone cluster of golfers who looked like they meant business. Feeling bold as brass, I approached the group, and in my most enthusiastic voice I enquired if any of them needed a caddie. To my eternal surprise, one of them looked me up and down and answered in the affirmative. My new boss simply told me to "stand by this bag," which seemed to be something I was more than qualified to do. The course went quiet, and there was a perceptible tension in the air as the players prepared to tee off. So, this was it. He and his partner would play a round of golf, and I would be their caddie. It was going to be an interesting, untaxing, and profitable day.

All went well for the first shots, as I trundled along behind the professional and his amateur buddy. Then one of them hit a ball into the rough—history doesn't relate whether it was the pro or the amateur. A search for the missing ball began, and eager to be seen as plucky, motivated, and proactive, I earnestly joined in. As others looked about fruitlessly, my heart skipped a beat when I saw, like a bird's egg in the grass, *the ball*.

With a spontaneous and unrehearsed flourish, I grabbed the ball and held it aloft. With all the heroism of Mel Gibson in *Braveheart,* I declared in as manly a voice as possible, "I found it!" before dropping it into the hand of the dumbstruck golfer.

"Have you *ever* caddied before?" he thundered, a perceptible lump in his throat.

3

"Do you know *anything* about golf?" he continued, not needing an answer.

So there I was, fired from my job less than thirty minutes after securing it. And then began my walk of shame down the fairway in a semi-daze. To add insult to injury, another guy from my school found an opportunity to assert his superiority at my expense.

"Get the f*** off the fairway! People are teeing off!"

Several thousand pairs of eyes were fixed on me and my shame that day, but that was nothing compared to the five hundred stares that greeted me when I arrived at school the following Monday. The school principal, Brother Miniter, walked straight up to me with a knowing expression on his face and asked:

"How was your weekend, Sebastian?"

I had confirmed for him what he had been saying repeatedly over the previous two years: I was stupid. And behind him, the five hundred gloating pairs of eyes waited for me to open my mouth and insert my own foot into it.

I don't know what spirit of genius possessed me, but from somewhere in my fear and embarrassment came the words:

"You'll never believe what I did..."

I went on to tell the story of how I had plummeted from hero to zero in a mere thirty minutes. Certainly I was being self-deprecating, but I really didn't expect the response I got. The dreaded principal smiled, rubbed my head, and declared:

"Ah, sure, it could have happened to a bishop."

As he said it, the five hundred faces fell to laughing—not laughing at me, but laughing at the story. Somehow, by taking ownership of the story, I moved from being the butt of the joke to being the storyteller—from being the victim to being the clown. In doing so, I learned two valuable things. First, I learned the power of vulnerability, and how, by showing your openness and honesty, you can make people like you and trust you. Second, I learned the power of stories as a way to communicate that vulnerability and a great deal more.

As a teenager, I discovered the power of stories to make people laugh or even just to pay attention. A night out with friends would be transformed from the mundane to the magnificent as soon as the stories began to flow. Relating an event, whether it be a football match or a date, went from a mere statement of facts to a drama involving an elaborate set-up, increasing tension and curiosity, and a satisfying conclusion.

While I'm not suggesting that I am one of the world's great raconteurs, I can honestly say that stories have helped me socially in numerous ways—from meeting new people, to engaging girls in conversation, to calming down tense or volatile situations. However, as a young man, I still only viewed the story as a social and entertainment device. I never considered the role or value of storytelling in a professional context until I was well into my adulthood—indeed, well into my professional career.

The catalyst that brought about this change in perception was the movie *Amistad,* released in 1997. I knew little about it before I saw it, but it had all the ingredients for a good historical film: major drama, an excellent director (Steven Spielberg), and a brilliant cast that included Anthony Hopkins and Morgan Freeman.

In a nutshell, *Amistad* is based on the story of a slave mutiny that took place aboard the Spanish-Cuban slave ship *Amistad* in 1839 and the complex legal battle that followed its capture by a US Revenue-Marine ship off the Long Island coast.

This was a mere twenty-two years before the American Civil War and the abolition of slavery, so the divide between those who opposed slavery and those who favored the status quo, was widening. In that sense, the actual mutiny aboard the *Amistad* was a catalyst for divisive debates taking place on shore. Some wanted the slaves punished and then either returned to their "owners" or executed as an example; others wanted them freed and sent home to Africa. Put it this way: if there had been TV at the time, this case would probably have taken up more airtime than the O. J. Simpson trial.

The drama of the movie moves to Washington, DC, where we encounter former President John Quincy Adams, played by Anthony Hopkins with his usual flair. While strolling in the gardens outside the House of Representatives, Adams is introduced to two of the country's leading campaigners for the abolition of slavery: an elderly, freed slave named Theodore Joadson, a fictional character played by Morgan Freeman; and Christian activist Lewis Tappan, played by Stellan Skarsgård. Both of them are successful shipping magnates in New England, and together they run a pro-abolitionist news-sheet called the *Emancipator*.

Having heard the plight of the *Amistad* Africans, Joadson and Tappan try to enlist the support of Adams, who, apparently verging on senility, refuses to help, claiming that he neither condemns nor condones slavery. They talk further, and in a courteous and eloquent manner, Joadson tries again to persuade Adams:

Joadson: Mr. President, if it was you handling the case…

Adams: (interjecting) But it isn't me, and thank God for that!

Joadson: (persisting) But if it was, sir, what would you do?

Adams: Well, when I was an attorney, a long time ago, young man…I realized after much trial and error, that in the courtroom, whoever tells the best story wins.

Whoever tells the best story wins.

The movie continued and the story unfolded, but to be honest, I can't remember what happened next. That phrase:

> "Whoever tells the best story wins," was taking a tour of my brain
> and shaking hands with every other thought it met!

As I began applying the tool of storytelling to various aspects of life, I realized that John Quincy Adams, 170 years ago, had spoken an ultimate truth—or maybe it was the twentieth-century scriptwriter putting that truth to his lips. Either way, it didn't take long for me to apply the technique to selling. In truth, the sales spiel is already a story: it has characters, a beginning, and an ending (and making a sale is a happy ending for most of us).

But what about the more subtle details of the sales process? Can a story be used to build trust with a prospect? Already, most of us use stories of other customers' experiences to further our cause, but could stories be used to identify a prospect's pain? Would a story make the dreaded "money conversation" any easier? What about stories that help to overcome objections or present solutions?

These thoughts were all gathering momentum in my mind as the credits rolled. Then the commercial break began, and I found myself being eyeballed by Dustin Hoffman in a promo for Sky Movies. It was as if he had been reading my mind. He looked me in the eye and spoke to me; I could almost hear him say, *Hey, Seb.*

> "Stories?" Dustin said. "We spend our lives telling them—about this, about that, about people. But some—some stories are so good we wish they'd never end. They're so gripping that we'll go without sleep just to see a little bit more. Some stories bring us laughter, and sometimes they bring tears, but isn't that what a great story does? Makes you feel? Stories that are so powerful"—he paused dramatically—"they really are with us forever."

7

His message rang in my ears: stories make you feel.

I'm not a big man for religious experiences, but being preached to by Anthony Hopkins and Dustin Hoffman is about as close as it gets.

Since then, the notion of stories that help us win and stories that make us feel has grown and grown for me. When we are in a sales situation, aren't we getting prospects to *feel?*

Let me put it another way. If a purchasing decision was purely a matter of facts and statistics with no "feelings" involved, there would never have been a need for sales teams to hit the road. If it were as simple as all that, we could just write to prospects and tell them the vital facts, and they would go and buy our product from the corner store.

But it has never been that way.

The whole sales cycle involves feeling, from the TV commercial for a chocolate bar to the multimillion-dollar contract. In each case, we are getting prospects to "feel":

- To feel good about us, the salesperson

- To feel comfortable about being vulnerable in our presence. After all, in many cases we're asking a prospect to admit to a problem— whether it's a personal problem, a business challenge, or a financial issue

- To feel their own dissatisfaction. If we are to remove their pain, we need them to feel it first

- To feel motivated enough to change. There won't be much chance of a sale if our prospect is prepared to go on tolerating their pain

Yes, John Quincy Adams and his scriptwriter were right. The best story wins—and not just in the courtroom. The story that best evokes the four feelings above is the story that wins the heart of the prospect—and with it, the sale.

Of course, it's no secret that people's motivations to buy are emotional. It's emotion that drives humans to avoid or overcome "pain," and the salesperson must find that pain. What I now see very clearly is that if a prospect is emotionally engaged, I can identify his or her pain more easily. And that's the age-old problem everyone involved in selling has to deal with. No matter how well you've mastered the selling system, the strategies, and the tactics, trying to get a prospect emotionally involved is like trying to spread cold butter on fresh bread.

You look at the two—your prospect and your product—your bread and your butter, in many ways. As a salesperson, you know they will go so well together. You know they were made for each other. But if you go about it the wrong way, if you are too rushed, you'll end up ruining the moment and losing the sale—or creating a sticky ball of dough and hard butter.

And this was my light bulb moment. If trying to get a prospect to emotionally engage is like attempting to spread cold butter on fresh bread, storytelling is like warming the butter first. With the right amount of storytelling, your message can be easily and successfully applied to your prospect.

The application of stories to sales situations just continues to grow the more you look at it. We all know the problem of trying to be remembered ahead of our competitors—and remembered for the right things.

There are many things you can do to be remembered. You can wear brightly colored shirts, bring doughnuts every time you meet a prospect, dye a purple stripe through your hair, or pull a Tom Cruise and jump up and down on a couch, declaring undying love for your prospect. Most of these are pretty shallow, and I particularly counsel you against trying the last one. (It might have worked for Tom, but it's not going to work for you.)

Joking aside, there are ways of being remembered that are gimmicks, and there are ways of being remembered that have substance. Being remembered as the guy with the *"Dennis the Menace* tie" is well and good, but wouldn't you rather be remembered for the conversations you have had? Sure, you can say clever and useful things and then hope to be remembered. But if you are able to convey your message in a story—a story with a setting, characters, a plot, and an ending or resolution that depends on your product or solution—then you have succeeded and will be remembered. You can recite a list of ten feature benefits and most of them will be easily forgotten, but if you weave them into a story where somebody's pain goes away because of those benefits, then they become integral to your product and the prospect's reason for wanting to buy.

When I was having my conversion moment with Sir Anthony Hopkins and Dustin Hoffman, I didn't know—but I have since learned—that this has been scientifically tested. The London School of Economics, whose alumni roster reads like a who's who of the good and the great—George Bernard Shaw, John F. Kennedy, and Mick "the lips" Jagger, to name but a few—conducted research into the efficacy of storytelling as a tool of persuasion. They discovered, among other things, that a message delivered via presentation had a 5–10 percent retention rate, but the same message delivered via a story had a 65–75 percent retention rate. This was corroborated by Chip and Dan Heath in their book 'Made to Stick: Why Some Ideas Survive and Others Die'. They got students to deliver one-minute speeches which included a fixed amount of statistics. In cases where stories were used, 63% of the class remembered the details, only 5% where the facts were given without a story. There are more studies out there, but already you can see that stories are a very effective tool for emotionally engaging a prospect and for being remembered afterward.

Since the days of the Kodak slide carousel presentation, business has been bewitched and enthralled by presentation technology. Certainly PowerPoint has its place—I'm not disputing that. The trouble is that we use this type of technology as a substitute for real engagement. We use it to do a job that can only be done effectively by ourselves. When we load up a presentation, we inevitably fill it with data—those ten feature benefits I mentioned before. But customers don't want data. They are up to their tonsils in data, and they are drowning in it. Aside from already having loads of it, the reason they don't want data is that it doesn't really tell them anything. Length, breadth, height, volume, speed, energy consumption, output, capacity, voltage, and memory—all of these measurements, along with their accompanying trial results, do nothing to show the customer how you are going to take their pain away. What customers and prospects crave is belief and faith—belief in you and what you have to offer them, and faith in the insights you have shared. PowerPoint presentations, websites, and video presentations can't convey this. Data can't demonstrate this. Only you can.

I'm willing to bet you have never heard anyone say that "facts move mountains." However, you don't have to be particularly religious to have heard the phrase:

"faith moves mountains."

But faith needs a powerful story to believe in—one that arouses and sustains conviction. A meaningful, sincere story that inspires people to believe in you and trust that you will deliver on your promise.

And that's another exciting element to this jigsaw, my friends, because when people believe what you say and trust your promise, you have *influence*. And believe me, influence is so much more memorable than the colored shirt, the bag of doughnuts, or the Tom Cruise antics.

Genuine influence goes deeper than getting people to do what you want them to do. True influence means people pick up where you left off because they believe.

Jesus, Gandhi, and Dr. Martin Luther King Jr. all inspired people to pick up where they left off. The tools of their trade? Stories. The same could be said of Mother Teresa and Nelson Mandela, and you could easily get the idea that there's something saintly in all of this, but these are tools and techniques that can be used by anyone. There is no doubt that Hitler,

11

Mussolini, Mao Tse-tung, and Stalin used the same techniques. And people have picked up where they left off.

There are many inspirational leaders and teachers in the business world. In the sales arena, David Sandler immediately comes to mind as someone whose memorable stories have engaged and inspired me, but there are many other examples. Anyone who follows the online series TED Talks knows that there are many great storytellers out there. In this book, I will focus on how you can use storytelling to your advantage and empower your sales journey.

Storytelling is your path to not only creating belief in yourself but also generating belief in others. Rather than giving customers a bundle of facts or statistics that they *must believe*, you tell a meaningful story that inspires them to reach the same conclusions you have reached and then to decide for themselves. That's because—and it'll seem obvious when I say it—people value their own conclusions more highly than anyone else's.

People believe in a story when it becomes real for them personally. If you can tell a story that people adopt as their own, you have earned their belief and trust. You have tapped into the powerful force of conviction. This is the universality of stories. When we believe them and they move us, we take them as our own, but we also remember where we heard them. Just as I remember my televisual epiphany with Messrs. Hopkins and Hoffman.

Once you have won belief and trust, you have also won heart and mind. If the prospect is someone with whom you will possibly have an ongoing relationship, you are now an influence in that person's life. Staying high in that prospect's estimations from here on out will require very little follow-up from you. Indeed, your influence may even expand as more people recall and retell your story to others.

As we explore the concept of stories, we will discover that stories are not always of the "once upon a time…happily ever after" variety. Our lifestyles and our actions are a part of our stories. If, while talking to a prospect in his or her office, you rescue a trapped butterfly and open a window to set it free, you may not have told a story verbally, but you have told a story about yourself. And whether your story is told through your actions or your words, you will not gain influence until you first secure the customer's trust.

Imagine if you were to say to prospects:

"Trust me, I'm a salesman."

Would their reaction be, "OK, I will"? I don't think so. Now imagine the power of hearing them saying—to themselves or to someone else—"I trust that salesman." That is a very powerful statement and is likely to yield commercial results.

And how do we get a prospect to say:

"I trust her!"

Well, let me tell you a story...

THE SPOKES-MAN

Mentors appear in unexpected places. Sometimes things – and people – have to be taken out of context before we can see them clearly.

There's a line from a song—I don't know who sings it—that says:

> "When you run away from one thing, you're running towards another."

It's always stuck with me. I remember it anytime I'm battling with a problem. It reminds me that giving up might yield bigger challenges.

> "Better the devil you know…"

This lyric ran through my mind as I paused at the intersection of my street and the main road. The peace of the cool spring morning contrasted with the throaty rumble of the Harley-Davidson beneath me, giving me a tingle—a sense of freedom. Now, we know that to get the sense of release that freedom gives us, we have to shed some burden or push some barrier away. So the question was, what was I free from? Was I running away from something? If so, what was I heading towards?

It was too early in the morning to consider such deep questions. Suffice it to say that I was delighted to be escaping from work for a couple of days. But escaping mentally is easier said than done. Looking forward as I was to the weekend ahead, my mind couldn't help but slip back into work mode. Working "in sales" brings its own unique pressures—pressures that on-lookers to the sales game just don't get. In sales you're only as good as the last deal you've done, and past victories are no guarantee of future success.

In sales. these two words cover an absolute ocean of industries, services, processes, systems, and occupations. *In sales* could mean selling uranium-tipped military hardware to emerging third-world nations. It could mean stocking gumball machines at truck stops. It could mean selling animal feed to cattle farmers or animal waste to vegetable farmers. On the one hand, *in sales* is an insultingly simplistic way of describing what you and I do. On the other hand, there's a certain purity about it because it defines our contribution to the businesses we serve. We are the people who "get it over the bar." Production staff can invent, design, and make a product; logistics can get it to the customer's door; accountants can get the money in. But if that magic moment between product and customer—the sale— doesn't occur, they're all out of a job.

A rush of adrenalin headed out to the four corners of my body as the reas-suring, virile pull of my Harley's 103 cubic-inch engine pulled me out onto the main thoroughfare. The motorcycle banked thirty degrees around the corner. *Yes!* The space left by whatever I was leaving behind was filled with the thrill and anticipation of spending three days exploring the hills with five other like-minded bikers.

You've probably already identified me as one of those midlife-bikers: mort-gage under control, kids increasingly independent, and for the first time in several decades, room in my mind to ask myself what it's all about. You would be right. About two years ago, over dinner with my wife, I said:

"Honey, I'm at that age."

From the look on her face, she was either expecting me to come out of the closet or disclose something medical and irreparable. With her lip slightly quivering, she asked:

"What age?"

"The age where I either get a mistress or a motorcycle," I replied.

"What's it to be?"

Oh, to have captured the look on her face. It was a delightful mixture of relief, love, and fury. As she moved towards forgiving me, we talked about it, and I reassured her about all the inevitable safety concerns. She is such a wonderful combination of reason and passion. All of her misgivings were based on her fear of losing me in some collision, but she heard me out, and now my biking weekends are marked on the calendar in the kitchen along with the kids' dental appointments and her mother's visits. Sometimes I even get lucky and her mother's visits coincide with my weekend rides!

Does it matter what sort of sales I'm in? I'm not sure that it does. What does matter is, I've moved into a different realm. I'm now up against the big guys. It's business-to-business, high ticket, high margin, and low prospect numbers. My competitors are sophisticated, and—worse still—they have good products. It would be so much easier if their products were substandard, but, as I've always said, life's a ball game—good competition makes for a good game. But this was where my anxiety lay. I'd proved that I was worthy of the challenges and rewards my new position was giving me, but did I have the tools to operate in this new environment? The more I used the same tools I'd been using for years, the blunter they seemed to get. It was ironic. A catch-22. A contradiction. I knew I was as good as they come, but I wasn't doing as well as I knew I should be.

As I left familiar streets, shops, fields, and hills behind me and followed the schoolmistress tones of "Sabrina," my satnav, I tried to erase these defeatist thoughts from my mind. I was behaving like my kids used to behave about their studies. They would insist that they could do it all later after the game, after the TV show, after dinner. My wife and I would always smile knowingly and reel them in. Now here I was, "running away" for a weekend with the boys, leaving my career up on blocks, promising to fix it after my return. Deep down, I knew that things were going to change over the weekend. Rationally, I know that if you turn your attention away from a problem for a while, your mind goes to work on it in the backroom of your brain. On a more superstitious level, I had a very strong inclination—an instinct—telling me that something was going to happen. I didn't know what—just something.

Somewhere between the blacktop and the horizon, I passed through an invisible barrier that rinsed the last of my cares away. It was as if a bit of my mind had left the house later than the rest of me and had now caught up. Now all of my attention was here, astride 103 cubic inches of semi-customized steel and alloy.

Why did I buy a Harley-Davidson instead of a different brand? Some people are born with engine oil under their fingernails; they grow up putting engines and machines together and actually know what all the pieces do. These are people whose knowledge of the performance and nuances of each machine is so profound that they would pick a different bike for each journey if they could. Those of us who are later converts to the sacred order of the bike choose our mounts in a completely different but no less complex way. Having spent the first half of my life on four wheels, graduating from Mazda to BMW, I knew and cared little about what went on beneath the hood, so long as the car did what I asked it to do. But the badge was important to me. It said I knew a good car when I saw one. It said I could afford to buy a good car when I wanted one. It gave me membership to a group marked:

"success and achievement."

So what values was I buying into by choosing a Harley-Davidson, a one-hundred-year-old motorcycle brand whose product quality and business success has fluctuated for over half its existence? Since 1969 it's gone from boom to bust as a corporation—it's had revivals and declines, it's had labour

18

problems, and it's had its ass whipped by Japanese imports. If you're going to look on the negative side of the Harley-Davidson scale, there's a lot of baggage. But one fact outweighs all of the negatives: Harley-Davidson is an icon. It's a black sheep leading a flock of would-be individuals. There is a contingent that wants space—physical and psychological—to call their own, and their way of getting it is through Harley-Davidson. Those two words tell a million stories—a million stories that involve the same hero and the same type of adventures. Like Batman, Captain America, or the Lone Ranger, Harley-Davidson always wins in the end. Like your favourite football or baseball team, Harley-Davidson is something you buy into and love—sometimes even at the expense of logic.

There had been no question about my choice. I am not a Goldwing man. Nothing's wrong with them—they're great bikes. I used to know a minister in his sixties who drove one, and he was passionate about it. He went to gatherings called "Wing Dings." And I've already told you how I feel about BMW, but it's the ones with four wheels on the ground that work for me. The rebel freedom of two wheels and the open road runs counter to the businesslike, Teutonic conformity of BMW. In my mind's eye, if you were to have a group of three guys touring on a Goldwing, a BMW, and a Harley, their night-time stops would look something like this: the Goldwing owner would be sitting by the fire reading a literary novel; the BMW owner would be looking at the map of tomorrow's journey; and the Harley-Davidson owner would be undoing and tightening nuts and squirting oil just to pass the time while taking cool, satisfying swigs on a longneck beer. Like the Harley ad says:

Some of us believe in the man upstairs.

All of us believe in sticking it to the man down here.

We believe in the sky and we don't believe in the sunroof.

We believe in freedom.

19

Yes, I suppose you could say I had bought into the fantasy, but is it really a fantasy? It's not just a bike, it's a story, and this is the episode I'm starring in. My Harley. My journey. My way.

By now I had turned off the motorway, or freeway, and the road became narrower and more twisted on its path up into the mountains. We had agreed to meet at 11 a.m. at a viewpoint car park. This would give each of us reasonable time to get there from our respective homes while still giving us a decent stretch of riding before the sun set—at which point we would all take out the longnecks and spanners and set to some bolt turning, and maybe a spot of whittling for good measure. Sabrina the satnav was still directing me, and it seemed I was getting pretty close. I now moved into the third phase of my journey's thinking. There is no better place to think than on the seat of a moving motorcycle. I am not joking when I say that it works on the same principle as chanting a mantra, saying a rosary, or swinging worry beads. The vibration calms you to the core. The consistent drone of the engine masks all other sounds. Your senses and thoughts align like a laser.

During the first part of the journey, my mind had been looking back on what I'd left behind. Then I was completely immersed in the journey and the bike. Now my thoughts projected towards my destination. I had made good time. It was a cool day, but it was bright and clear. I would be more than happy to arrive at the viewpoint before the others and continue my meditation there. I know the place, and there are few spots that inspire as much awe.

I already knew three of the guys I would be meeting, having met them at previous Harley-Davidson chapter meetups. Cormac is a long-distance truck driver. The key to his marital success seems to be spending two weeks driving to the Ukraine and back, arriving home, doing his laundry, and then touring elsewhere on his bike. I'm surprised he can remember his children's names—or that he was even around long enough to conceive them—but hey, let's not go there. Alan is an academic—his field has something to do with political history, I believe. His life consists mostly of reading and giving lectures, with occasional appearances on TV discussion panels.

Antonio is an Italian chef. I have heard great things about what he can do over a campfire, and something tells me he won't be wasting time with the spanner and the longneck.

The two men I don't know are Shaun and Jack. Shaun recently joined the club, and Jack is a former senior vice-president of an American corporation that bought him back on as a consultant to sort out their European operation. I looked him up, and he's impressive. I checked the usual networking and professional sites, but it was the general searches that brought up the most interesting nuggets. He is the man they send in to revive and revitalise flagging operations and divisions, and wherever he goes, stock goes up. From what I could see he hadn't been to college, but he had worked in just about every area of business, from production to accounts to sales. I was thinking about how much I was looking forward to meeting him as I pulled into the viewpoint's car park. There, ahead of me, was a very customised, battle-worn, but proud hawg. No, this wasn't your regular Harley-Davidson—that sounds too stiff and upright. It was a 100-percent blue-collar hawg. I pulled up beside it, switched off my engine, and took off my helmet, resting on the seat for a moment to take in the unfamiliar silence, the cool breeze, and the astonishing view. I stayed in a trance for quite some time before I eventually swung my stiff right leg over the gas tank. It was only when I opened up the pannier to get something out that it occurred to me: there was nobody around to go with the remarkable machine I had parked alongside. Even if the owner had gone behind a rock to relieve himself, he would have been back before now. I poured a cup of coffee from my flask and went to sit on the wall, my feet dangling above the valley far below. I sank back into my solitary reverie; the skittering clouds overhead stroked my soul. Suddenly, a booming voice echoed across the landscape, sending my heart into my mouth and coffee all over my leathers. I nearly fell off the wall.

"View's much better from up here!" said the voice.

"Holy shit," I whispered angrily, as my heart retreated back down my throat. I praised my own foresight in packing extra underwear. I slowly swivelled my head around, determined to maintain my cool and not let him know how much he had rattled me. On the other side of the road from the car park, the hillside rose precipitously upward, and there, about fifty feet above me, was a stocky, weathered-looking man with a trim, grey beard, a full head of wavy hair, a weathered complexion, and the hooded brow of someone who has spent a lot of time scrunching up their eyes against sunlight and wind.

"Well, the fall is considerably less from down here," I replied.

After saying that, I got up, placed my thermos cup on my bike seat, and went over to the seemingly vertical rock face where he sat. I was taking a gamble, as I had no idea how he'd climbed to the top. I could easily have ended up making a fool of myself. But without too much effort or loss of dignity, I scrambled up to where he sat.

"Seb," I wheezed, slumping down on the turf beside him.

"Jack," he said, his eyes still fixed on the extraordinary view.

He was right; the view was better from where we were sitting, partly because we were set in far enough not to see the road. No signs of human interference spoiled the spectacular valley that unfolded beneath us.

It was at this point that I realised he hadn't been able to see me arriving or sitting on the wall. He had heard the motorcycle and surmised, from its throaty rumble, that it was probably a Harley, and that I was, therefore, a member of the group. That didn't make him Sherlock Holmes, I admit, but I still found him a bit of a smart-ass. We were half an hour ahead of the agreed meeting time, which meant we could be sitting here for up to forty-five minutes before anyone else turned up. I quashed any possible irritation I might have felt and rummaged around in my mind for a conversation starter. I went in at the shallow end first.

"I'm guessing from your bike that this isn't your first ride-out. When did you start biking?"

"Can't remember a time I didn't have a Harley," he said reflectively, as if he was trying to recall some distant point in his childhood where he graduated from stroller to hawg.

"What about you?"

"I bought a scooter at eighteen. Not really a bike—more of a glorified lawnmower."

I paused. His facial expression hadn't changed, and I figured I ought to close the gap between the scooter and the shiny-new machine parked alongside his veteran, road-wise, custom bike.

"I bought the Harley just over a year ago," I said.

He shook his head slowly and whistled through his teeth.

"Wow! Your first bike, and it's a Softail?" He laughed.

"Oh, that's not my first bike," I blurted.

"I got my first proper bike about eighteen months ago. A Harley Sportster—the 883 Superlow."

"Nice bike," he said unconvincingly.

"What happened to it?"

I could see the cogs in his mind turning. Six months was hardly any time at all to own a bike. If I'd written it off in an accident I wouldn't have been graduating to something twice the size.

"I traded it in to buy the Softail Heritage. I tell you, you're going to think I'm a really sad SOB when you hear why."

As soon the words left my mouth, I was already wondering what in the world had made me say them.

"Shoot!" he said, more enthusiastically.

"Well," I began, "I'd had the Superlow about four months. It was running really well—like a dream. No problems at all."

"But?" he interjected.

"One Saturday afternoon, I dropped by the Harley-Davidson dealership and I got to chatting with a true-blue, traditional Harley dude. You know the type…perfectly combed beard like one of the guys in ZZ Top."

"A fellow pilgrim and road warrior. I know them well."

He smiled.

"We were talking about this and that. Mainly we were talking about the models on display and referring back to the previous models they'd evolved from. He mustn't have seen me arrive because, eventually, he asked what sort of bike I rode. I pointed to the 883 Superlow."

I paused for effect before continuing.

"He nodded knowingly and said, 'Good choice. That's a great beginner's bike. I got one for the wife a while back. Can't get her off it.'"

Jack was looking me in the face, interested and evidently unable to guess what the conclusion of my anecdote would be.

"I admit it, Jack. That was it for the 883. Two months later I had swapped it for that baby down there."

He laughed at my self-deprecation, but I could see from his reaction that he agreed with the Harley dude about the Superlow 883.

"Do you put many miles on it?" he asked.

"Not as many as I'd like. Not much opportunity during the week, but these weekends are fantastic. They're a great way of—metaphorically and literally—leaving behind all the shit life throws at you."

I had expected him to ruminate and ponder. He seemed like the sort of guy who would stare off into the distance for a minute or two before replying—the type to leave you hanging. So, I was taken aback when he responded almost immediately.

"Are you sure you've left it behind you?"

Yes, I was a bit surprised by his question, although I wasn't sure whether it was because of his blunt delivery or the fact that he seemed to know the answer.

"What line of business are you in?" he asked dispassionately.

"I'm in sales," I said.

He responded quickly, surprising me again.

"Ah, so you're a storyteller!" he replied.

I was genuinely puzzled, but he didn't leave me much time to think.

"What d'you sell?"

"I sell software that helps corporations and large organisations speed up order entry and reduce processing costs" He looked interested, so I continued…. "We do this by making order-entering capability remote and putting it in the hands of the sales force. We link up manufacture, distribution, supply, and sales."

I had this speech well practiced. It was enough to cover the subject without sending people to sleep.

"Well," he said, "isn't that a story of sorts? It could do with a bit more belief and excitement, but it is a story."

"I suppose it is," I said, still a bit puzzled. "I don't see it hitting the bestsellers lists, but I guess it is a story."

"Trouble is, you've told that story too many times," he said, pulling at a bush near his feet.

"That's always the challenge, trying to find new ways of telling that same old 'we can help you' story."

A moment ago I had been irritated by his clever-clever, know-it-all attitude. Now I felt a wave of comfort—that's the only way to describe it. In one sentence, Jack had described my dilemma. I had moved to a different area of sales; I was targeting a different customer base. I needed a new way to express what I was offering so that a new group of people could identify with my words and be convinced by my message.

I laughed, shaking my head.

"You couldn't have put it better if I'd spent an hour telling you my story, if you'll pardon the pun."

He smiled. It was a good, warm smile that smoothed out any of the feathers he had previously ruffled.

"Well, don't take an hour over it, buddy, but why not tell me how you got to where you are? Listen to yourself tell it and you'll probably hear the answer. I might even make a suggestion or two myself along the way."

So there we were, fifty vertical feet above our bikes, which were parked five hundred feet above the valley floor, as I began my story.

Over a period of fifteen years, I had changed companies twice, making several significant steps up the ladder within each. I had always managed to meet and exceed targets. I also strived for consistency. I was never comfortable with having a spectacular, record quarter and then not being able to replicate that success. Better to consistently be a bit ahead than to see the graph peak and trough.

Now I was at a crossroads in life and work. I needed to keep working, but my goals and needs were different. My current employer had recognised my success, experience, and seniority by granting me a new role—one that offered a significant increase in potential earnings. But somehow, I felt like a David facing Goliath. The sophisticated weaponry of my competitors dwarfed my tired, outmoded toolbox.

"What you've got to remember about David and Goliath," Jack said, pausing for effect, "is that David won!"

I laughed, reflecting on this. Jack was right, of course. It's having the belief in yourself, as you go into the fray, that wins you the day. Doubt is self-fulfilling.

I went on. I have always described myself as a "driven person"—one who's driven by a careful driver. In other words, I have taken enough risks to make life interesting, but I've never bet the house on anything.

"Tell me," Jack said, pulling a sprig of heather out of the turf and studying the little mauve flowers along the stem.

"Do you play any sport?"

27

"Golf," I said.

He smiled a very genuine smile saying, almost under his breath.

"I guess golf is a sport, come to think of it. What level do you play at?"

"I don't embarrass myself too often," I replied.

I wouldn't describe myself as boastful, but I do play a good game of golf. Trophies have accumulated to the point that my wife is no longer proud of me for winning them. She has banished them to the kids' rec room.

"Were you born playing golf? I mean, isn't golf scoring stepped so that you make your way up the ladder as your game improves?"

Answering his first question, I said:

"No, I wasn't. I worked hard at it. My competitive streak is less disguised in sport than it is in business."

That thought had never occurred to me before then, but it was true. I had always made a point of behaving in a courteous and cooperative way in the work environment—even with competitors. Mostly it's just the way I was brought up—civility was a big thing with my mother. Over time, however, I'd honed that civility and incorporated it into my arsenal. It disarms people who expect you to come in all:

"carpetbags and snake oil." Instead, they find a relaxed, calm atmosphere.

These days I realise, however, that whatever the sport, I want to win. I'm not nasty about it or anything, it's just how I see things. Work is ongoing. It's forty to sixty hours of your week, through thick and thin, good and bad. You need to balance your energies and manage your relationships. Sport is another matter. There's a defined time around a game, just as there are lines around the pitch. But what was the point he was trying to make?

> "So you've graduated your way through the golf ranks to get where you are. You've been the David golfer among the Goliath golfers. You just haven't noticed because you've been focusing on how your game has improved, not on the other players. Maybe that's what you need to do now."

He was right. When you practice your swing, your eye follows the ball from the tee to the hole. If you're watching the other players, you're going to miss hitting the ball. But he was getting a bit academic and theoretical. I protested.

> "There isn't any comparison between my golf game, my clients, and my competitors who want their business."

> "There's only a comparison if you make a comparison. And when you make that comparison, you control how they see you, your message, and your product."

Jack's voice is hard to describe. He speaks in an almost hushed tone in conversation. Instead of making it more difficult to hear him, it makes you pay more attention. I noticed this even more further into the trip. In groups of people he would speak at that low, quiet level, and everyone would just listen harder. It's ideal, really.

So there I was, listening intently so as not to miss a word of this virtual whisper. I heard every word, but I must admit I wasn't sure what he was driving at. The other guys were going to be there any minute, and, whatever this guy had to say, I wanted to hear it and understand it. Then I'd be in a position to either accept it or reject it. And the only way to bring things to a head was to deploy that much underused communication tool—the truth.

> "I'm sorry, you've lost me."

29

He laughed.

> "You've got to tell your truth your way. I'm just saying that if you look at your work situation and you see a comparison with your golf game, that's good material. And if you can use that comparison to tell your story and have people understand you better—do it. That's what I mean. If you make the comparison, you own the comparison."

I was finding his idea interesting, but it wasn't quite gelling with me yet.

> "My new work circumstances are simply another version of me moving into a tougher handicap level in golf? What's that got to do with my prospective clients?"

He looked at the sprig of heather again, tilting his head back and looking at it like a long-sighted doctor trying to read a thermometer.

> "You're not selling snake oil. You're not selling copier machines. You're in the big league. Before any of your people are going to bite, you will have eaten a lot of lunches together and drunk a lot of coffee. You are part of the equation. They're going to want to believe in you before they close a sale, and you've got to give them a story they can believe in."

He was right. A prospect who hears about my dogged determination at golf, my unimpeachable standards, or my supportiveness to friends and colleagues is going to get a picture of a man who is worth doing business with.

> "It's the stuff they pick up from the periphery of what you say that helps them build a picture. Anyone can sell a dental-perfect smile, a chiselled jaw, or a perfect haircut. It's the helpful gesture, the offhand smile, or the wink that gets the attention and the recall."

I wasn't going to tell him that I thought he was the clearest-thinking person I'd ever met. I thought I'd leave it at "you're making a lot of sense." I

30

really had a starting point now for where to take my new role. I stood up, stretched, and nearly lost my footing. My leg was still a bit asleep from the ride, and, combined with a touch of vertigo from seeing the view below me, I was a bit shaken. Jack was kind enough not to mention the sudden panic that pulsed through me like an electric shock. Instead, he stood, took a similar stretch, and began ambling towards the point where it was easiest to climb down to the road.

"I want to take a look at the bike now that it's cooled down. There was a strange noise coming from the front forks. That's the thing about a custom. More watching, more working."

I gave my leg a good flex before following him down to where our two bikes stood side by side. Sure, a Harley is a Harley at the end of the day, but now, looking at my trim, showroom-perfect Softail standing beside his weathered, custom Road King, I felt a bit green.

"That's some bike you've got there. Had it long?"

"I call her my second wife. After I got divorced, I was kind of restless. She took care of me, and we've been together ever since—that's twenty years. When they asked me to come over to Europe, that was the first thing I put in the contract: priority freight for my second wife. Got some funny looks, I tell you."

I would describe Jack as a man of few words, but his words delivered a lot. I now knew he had a soft and vulnerable side, he had a sense of humour, he'd been married and divorced, and he was an eccentric. He had introduced himself to me in a "good-cop, bad-cop" manner. First I'd seen the strong, resolute man of iron, now I was seeing his more tender, human side.

He was lying on the ground, looking up at the base of his bike. I leant back on my seat, cradling the now-cold coffee as I looked out at the view.

"So," I said. "If you were me, what would you do? How do you reckon I should approach my new selling role?"

31

"I guess your first step is to ask yourself why you do what you do—and I don't mean 'to feed the kids' or 'to make a buck.' It might sound strange, but those aren't the things that make us jump out of bed on a workday. There are plenty of guys with obligations who've gone crazy because their work made them unhappy."

Again, I hadn't thought about this. What parent can deny having those moments where they say:

"If it wasn't for these pesky kids, I'd be skydiving in Mexico, scuba diving in the Seychelles, or running a dental-floss farm in Montana"?

But the reality is, the vast majority of us are like volcanic ash, autumn leaves, and snow: we find a level and we settle on it. So, why was I in sales?

"You know, when I think about it, I can trace it back to when I was at school. I had my nerd side and my jock side. In sport I liked the combination of physical skill and psychological skill. When I was about fourteen, I came up with this theory about football. 'You can either run away from the other team, or you can use them to help you score.' If you have the ball and you're running towards the goal line, you can either see yourself as a fugitive with them chasing you, or a leader with them following you.

"I then realised that this is how martial arts works too. When Bruce Lee sees a kick coming, he can either see it as a force he has to stop before it hurts him, or a power for him to lead and direct to his advantage.

"Somewhere in all of this, I got into debating and ended up on the debating team. How? The same thing. I took the arguments and points others made against me, and, instead of simply countering them or undermining them, I systematically turned those arguments to my advantage. I suppose it's a variation on 'what doesn't kill me makes me stronger.'

"Now that you ask me why I'm in sales, there's the reason. I like steering the game, guiding the argument. I like the fact that it is both competitive and social. You get to the end of a successful sale cycle, you've closed, you shake hands—everyone's happy. Not like a boxing bout or a ball game where, even though you're shaking hands, somebody has lost."

He hadn't been looking my way, but I now realised he had been up on one elbow, spanner idle, as I said my piece.

"What was your question again?" he asked.

"My question?" I had to think for a moment before I remembered.

"It was, how do I approach my new sales role? How can I leave the 'shit' behind and enjoy my weekend with the boys?"

"Well, I say tell your prospects what you told me."

He was back worrying a few nuts with his socket set.

"You mean about debating, football, and martial arts?"

I laughed.

"What's that got to do with anything?"

"It's good material. I learned something—not just about you but also about stuff. You see, it's not just about what you're actually saying, it's about what they're hearing. It's not what you say, it's what they infer."

He could see I wasn't convinced. It was obviously still written on my face. He went on.

"Let me tell you a story, Seb. Early in my career, I worked as a sales rep for a software company. Hard to imagine it, but what we sold at the time was cutting edge. It involved twenty-two installation disks to get it up and running—three-and-a-half-inch floppy disks. Remember them?" He looked up.

"I try to forget them!" I replied.

"Well, it was a start-up company, about nine months old when I joined it. My role was business development, so I had to prospect and close business. We were selling to network operators around Europe, competing with the likes of AT&T and Cable & Wireless, so I had to work hard: a lot of cold calls, a lot of meeting prospects - demonstrations, presentations, frustrations!

"I was working hard and my intentions were good. I wanted to succeed and I wanted the company to do well. They'd taken a risk hiring me. I was the only sales guy in a start-up with zero customers and a bunch of our venture-capital backers on our backs baying for a return on their investment.

"Nine months in, I had an opportunity with a Scandinavian mobile company. They had a heap of legacy infrastructural technology that needed to be replaced. There was a lot of pain: good quantifiable pain, you know what I mean?"

I nodded. Those sorts of situations were great, except for the competing flock of vultures circling the carcass.

"I had two weeks to prove that our system was eligible before the real tendering began, so I was holed up in Oslo with a team of our engineers. I had it on good faith from my prospect that, if we passed 'proof of concept,' we'd be shortlisted with one other competitor. A 50-50 race? You've still got to fight, but it's an even field.

"When I told my boss back in the United States, he promised to erect a statue of me outside headquarters if I brought the business home. I was feeling great about this until one night when I was having a beer with Torstein, a seasoned sales guy with another software vendor—thankfully not in competition with me. In conversation, he mentioned that he had a purchase order for a quarter of a million dollars from the mobile company—when we were all still in our two-week proving period.

"It didn't make sense to me back then. Back then, I thought you earned the right to present by the sweat of your brow: doing presentations and jumping through hoops on the way to the negotiation table, where you would be broken down and humiliated by pack of rabid buyers. If you survived, there was a deal at the end of it. But now I'm talking to this guy who's won before he's begun!

"I had a good relationship with my prospect, so over a sandwich one day, I asked him straight out.

"Jan," I said. "I was talking with Torstein, and I kind of got the impression he already has a purchase order—ahead of proof of concept."

He smiled as if it was the most natural thing in the world and replied:

"Yes, Jack, that's right. He has a PO."

I was gobsmacked. All I could say was:

"How come?"

"What he said then will stay with me forever. I took it in at once, even though I was still processing what I believed to be a grave injustice. He said, "I guess he's just a really good sales guy."

"Seb, I'm not a violent man, I want you to know that. If I were, I'd probably be in a Scandinavian jail right now! I consoled myself that Torstein hadn't taken my piece of the business and that I was still lining up for a 50-50 race—unless there were more purchase orders doing the rounds.

"A couple of nights later, I arrived a few minutes late for dinner with Jan, my prospect, and Torstein, of purchase-order fame. One of them had obviously been telling a funny story, which they were polite enough to share with me. Apparently, IBM had come in on the project and offered their equivalent of Torstein's software to Jan's company—for free. A global company's product *free*, yet Jan and Torstein were here laughing their hearts out. I didn't understand.

"'So, Jan, you're still going to pay up a quarter of a million dollars when you could get the software free? I'm really happy for Torstein, of course, but how come?'

"He stopped laughing and looked across the table at me with a half smile. 'You know, Jack—nothing is for free. You're going to end up paying it one way or the other. With this guy,' he said, pointing to Torstein, 'I know how much I'm paying now. I know how he does business, and I know he will be there when I need him.'

"I had to admit to myself, there and then, that Torstein was an extremely good salesman. Not only had he secured a purchase order before the tender process had officially begun, he had also held onto his $250 million order where a competitor was offering an equivalent for free. I wanted some of what that guy had. Afterwards, I asked him to tell me his secret.

"He told me he told stories, which of course I knew. But, in addition to telling stories, he said the real secret was to pay attention to the stories your prospect was trying to tell you."

I was puzzled and asked Jack to explain.

"Think about it this way," Jack went on, "every story ever told has four key elements. Think of any novel you've ever read, any movie you've seen—they all had the same four elements: setting, complication, turning point, and resolution.

"The *setting* is where you are introduced to the characters and the background story. Then you witness some form of *complication*. The stability of the setting is shaken by some event that is either internally or externally generated—it could be anything from a kidnapping to an earthquake or a murder, an infidelity or an inheritance. It could even just be some kid leaving town to go to college, and the changes that brings to friends and family.

"At some point, the main character—or characters—comes to a *turning point*, where he has to face the changes and challenges brought about by the complication. Once he's faced those, the dominoes then start to fall in the direction of the *resolution*. Those are the four elements that make a story. I guarantee that if you tell a story and leave one of those steps out, your audience will be scratching their heads!

"I found that this was the exact same process my prospects went through every time they made a major investment. There was the world they lived in quite happily: the setting. Then came some sort of complication: a machine becomes obsolete, a new regulation means changes to a production line, or a competitor introduces new technology. If that complication is serious enough and affects enough of the right people, then there's going to be a turning point. Somebody's going to have to take their head out of the sand and make a decision about how to address the complication. From there on, all those who want to keep their jobs are praying for a 'happy ever after.' Presto! Resolution.

"When I thought about what Torstein was telling me, it made so much sense. I had done plenty of sales courses—some good, some bad—but they left me full of theory, which fell apart when I put it into practice. Torstein's notion of telling stories and listening to stories made a lot of sense. It was more conversational, more relaxed, and, as a result, more genuine and sincere.

"There were also a few logical extensions of this idea. If the prospect is telling a story, he isn't just giving you the setting, complication, and turning point, then looking to you for the resolution. He's also giving you the cast of characters: influencers, users, decision makers, doubters, and more. And by giving you all of these characters and their roles, you automatically know whom you are going to be up against throughout the rest of the project. It's almost like saying to a prospect: 'If this were a movie, who would the main stars be, and what will the budget be?' When it came to presenting my solution, all I had to do was re-run scenes from their movie.

"I adapted this approach to every sales opportunity I was involved in, and I quickly became the number-one rep. Not only was I outselling my competitors, I was working fewer hours. Selling became fun again. I reframed how I saw the selling role. Instead of trying to convince people we were better than everyone and that they needed us—something I was never comfortable with—I was now helping bring prospects' own stories to life and helping them to the right 'resolution' of their tale—personally and professionally."

I understood most of what he was saying. We'd had a sales guru come in and speak to our company not that long before. He had talked about stories and storytelling, but at the time, frankly, I'd been dismissive, much as Jack had been about the courses he'd attended. It was very different, however, to be hearing a process brought to life by an actual practitioner, who had seen his own fortunes turn by using the system. There was just one part that wasn't really working for me.

"OK, Jack, I'm with you so far on this," I said.

"There's just one bit I'm not clear on. What do you mean by getting prospects to tell their personal story?"

"Everyone is trying to tell a story to the world," he began.

Anyone else saying that would have sounded like a second-rate preacher, but somehow Jack struck the right balance.

"Think about it, Seb. What story were you trying to tell when you chose a Harley instead of a BMW or a Goldwing? Was it 'I'm still young,' 'I'm a rebel,' 'I've arrived,' 'I'm an independent thinker,' or 'I'm at a point in life where I don't care what other people think'?"

He didn't wait for an answer. It was as if he had already decided what sort of a biker I was.

"What about your watch? Cheap and cheerful? Functional and no attachment beyond the strap? Gold heirloom from Great Uncle Montgomery? Or one that's called an oyster even though it's the size of a giant clam? Watches, pens, ties, cars, bikes, cereals, beers, baked beans, and holiday destinations: they are all part of the story you're telling the world. They are all the threads you are weaving into the narrative of your life, a story that says, 'I worked hard. I made good choices. I've been successful at home and at work, and now I'm ready to enjoy that success.'"

He paused for a bit.

"Yes sir, we wear our stories like clothes until we open our mouths. Then we tell them. And don't kid yourself—we tell horror stories too. Unconsciously, we reveal untidy settings, avoidable complications, uncomfortable turning points, and undesirable resolutions—but that's for another day."

I was intrigued. I wanted to know how Jack the storytelling convert evolved into corporate, global Jack. So I asked him what had led him upward from the highly desirable and successful sales role he seemed to have created for himself.

"Well, as the company grew from a start-up with one customer to a major player, they recognised my role in that growth, so they did what all stupid companies do with their top sales talent—they made me a manager. In a heartbeat—and with a significant pay raise—I went from an environment I controlled, with forecasts I could predict and goals I could accurately set, to the guesswork department.

"My job was to create territory plans, second-guess forecasts, and put out fires. The reality was, I was over a group of people who were blundering around the field losing leads and failing to close sales that I would have reeled in blindfolded. My image and my bonuses were dependent on incompetent amateurs that I hadn't hired, couldn't fire, and couldn't retrain. I spent days in pointless meetings with fools talking their way through to cocktail hour so they wouldn't have to do any real work. It was all about being seen as busy, and that seemed to involve a lot of macho frowning and posturing. Effectively, I was sinking into a quagmire of testosterone."

"So, what did you do?" I asked.

"I was almost ready to quit when one night, in a hotel room on a trip, I found myself watching a show that is best described as a low-budget version of *The Apprentice* on cable. The host of the show was a guy called Bill Conlon, a self-made man and the eldest of fourteen kids, who ran a market stall from a very early age to help feed the family. How do I remember? It was a story, and he just kept on telling it. He left school at thirteen and went on to become a multimillionaire in the motor industry—amongst other businesses.

"Towards the end of the show, we saw him sitting there, all imperious, as he said to one contestant, 'Why shouldn't I send you home?' The contestant replies, 'You shouldn't fire me, Bill, because I have incredible determination and the drive to succeed. I admit that I left school early, but I did that because I was the eldest child and I came from a poor family and needed to earn money. I started my own business at eighteen, and despite my humble origins, I've overcome every obstacle.'

"Bill smiled at this, then turned to the other contestant, a former male model who was dressed in an immaculate three-piece suit. He asked him: 'Why shouldn't I send you home?'

"'Well, Bill," the man began, in a rather cocky fashion. 'You shouldn't fire me because I have a master's degree in marketing and entrepreneurship.'

"Who do you think he fired, Seb?"

"The guy with the master's?" My answer was hesitant. It seemed too obvious to be right. I would have done the same.

"Exactly, Seb. Exactly. The college kid had completely ignored the story Bill Conlon had told him, focusing instead on his own story—which was never going to impress a self-made man like Bill. The empathy, understanding, and synergy between Bill and the first guy were palpable. They were essentially telling the same story. There was nothing between Bill and the college kid. Knowing that their story has been heard is much more important to prospects than 'return on investment.'"

I'll admit, I was starting to wonder what the connection was between this TV programme and Jack's frustrations on being taken off the road and put in the head office.

"Seeing that show clearly demonstrated to me the importance of listening to the stories of others so I could be sure of telling the right story when it was my turn. I realised I had a choice of either quitting the managerial position and getting myself a sales job again or taking the bull by the horns. If I could help my reps tell their stories and learn to listen to their prospects' stories, I could get my job satisfaction back while having a massive impact on the lives of the reps—not to mention the company's bottom line. With that decision, with that reorientation, I went from being a disillusioned manager to being the lynchpin of each rep's story out in the field."

That was the jigsaw piece I'd been missing that connected the Bill Conlon anecdote to his job. As I let it sink in, I saw Jack watching me expectantly.

"So, Seb," he said. "Tell me, how much of that story is true?"

Why wouldn't it be true? I thought to myself. *Why would he make it up?* I guess the same reason Aesop made up fables, Jesus made up parables, and Uncle Remus told his stories. You make up a story to illustrate your point.

"A story can tell a truth without being true," I answered, quite proud of myself.

"Spot on," he said, smiling. "You're catching on. I could put my hand on my heart and say that everything I just told you happened, but not in the same time, in the same place, to the same people. I could just as easily set the story in London, for example, but that wouldn't make the anecdote, parable, fable—or whatever you want to call it—any less valid."

I was trying to remember back to what had prompted his stories about the Scandinavian mobile company and the TV show. True to his theory, I had thoroughly absorbed the points he was making, precisely because they had been communicated to me through the process of setting, complication, turning point, and resolution. I looked out at the view and tested myself on the last one—the one about the apprentice. Setting: Jack had been very successful at sales. Complication: his company had taken him off the road and made him a manager, which wasted his talents and dragged him down. Decisive moment: while watching a TV show, he recognised the power of listening to prospects' stories and empathising. Resolution: he set out to impart his skills and knowledge to his team of reps, achieving phenomenal results and great job satisfaction. If that had been given to me as disembodied data, without characters or a narrative, I wouldn't have taken it in, and I certainly wouldn't have remembered it.

What had I been telling him? This was all great stuff, but I'll be honest with you, I wanted to keep the focus on my issues in case I could get some good insights. We'd talked about David and Goliath and acknowledged the fact that David had won. Then I remembered.

"OK, a story doesn't have to be 'true'—it's a vehicle for conveying 'truth,'" I began in earnest. "In all likelihood, therefore, the stories we use in sales will be composites of real experiences—our own and those we've heard—or they'll be complete fantasies, like the *Tortoise and the Hare*, right?"

He nodded as I spoke.

"Back there," I went on, "you told me I should tell prospects how I was in high school—how I turned my thinking from being chased by opponents to leading them. How I liked sales because it was a game with two winners. What relevance does that have to my current business situation? How is that my new way to tell an old story?"

Noticing that my speech had come to an end, he ceased nodding and returned his attentions to the motorcycle.

"OK. You tell that story and you're opening yourself up. It's honest; it's heartfelt. What is your prospect hearing? What is he taking in?"

"Like I said, he'll think he's talking to a nerd," I answered.

"I guess," he began, "as I said earlier, it's about the peripheral vision. You tell them about an incident where you messed up and they're going to see a guy who faces up to his mistakes, learns from them, and tells the truth about them. There, in one fell swoop, you're already a one-in-a-hundred guy!"

He paused. There was a particularly stubborn nut to be undone.

"Values are something you can't tell as facts. Bet you've never gone into a meeting and said, 'Hey, Mr. Prospect, I'm your guy. You can trust me, I'm a salesman.' It's as if the act of saying it out loud makes it untrue. Same thing about mistakes. Tell someone that if you make a mistake you'll put your hand up, and it sounds like you're planning to fail. Always be thinking about what they're inferring—how is the tale you're telling being received and interpreted?"

Part of me was thinking that I didn't have it in me to tell stuff to people that way. I'd be too self-conscious. I'm a practical, facts man. Then I was glad I hadn't said this out loud, because, at this point, I could tell what the response would be, something like, 'You told it to me, didn't ya?' That being said, I still needed to explore this part of it.

"You say I should tell them about my football theory and so forth, right?"

"Well, yeah—but I don't mean tell the same story every time you're talking to a new prospect. There are times for telling personal stories about yourself, and then there are times for the third-party stories that begin with, 'I knew a fella once…' Stories are just different ways of telling the truth."

"Isn't that a kind of contradiction?" I laughed. "Stories being the truth?"

He got up on both elbows this time to emphasise his point. In fact, he was able to lift one hand up and wave his spanner in the air without losing his balance.

44

"Heck no, that's no contradiction. Why have Shakespeare's plays lasted? Because they're all full of truth. Why do parents still read their kids Winnie the Pooh? Because it's full of truth. *The Wizard of Oz, Bambi, It's a Wonderful Life, Oliver Twist, War and Peace*—all of them, full of truth. Just because truth is in your peripheral vision or in how you infer things, it doesn't make it a lie.

"You see, there's a difference between something being *true* and something being the *truth*. The saying, 'A stitch in time saves nine'—it's a *truth*, because if you don't fix something early, you're going to have a bigger job on your hands later on. But nobody is suggesting it's *true*. Nobody is saying that if you don't darn a sock at 11 a.m., by 11 p.m. you'll have nine times as many stitches."

I think I can safely say that, at this point, he was being quite passionate about his line of argument.

"From what you've told me directly and from what I've seen in my peripheral vision, I know you're experienced, thorough, professional, conscientious, efficient, and driven by targets and innovation. You haven't told me a single one of those things directly, but that's what I got—because you told me stories, not facts. That's what's going to set you apart."

He heaved himself up off the ground as if he was either going to punch me or give me a bear hug. It was a very flattering list of impressions he had recited, but it came across so naturally that I didn't feel in the least bit embarrassed and awkward. He sat astride his bike and was about to fire her up, but before doing so he added:

"Being understood and being remembered for the right reasons are two of the most valuable things in this world. Take out your phone and search the phrase, 'Leading provider of.' How many hits do you get?"

I did as he said, and in a matter of seconds I had the number he was looking for.

"Three hundred and twenty-eight million, and counting."

"OK, now read three of 'em."

I listed them off one, one by one:

Company A: Leading provider of vehicle remarketing services and has a full range of auction, reconditioning...

Company B: Leading provider of transformation and outsourcing services...

Company C: Leading provider of digital edition and digital archiving solutions...

It really is remarkable. Not just the amount of businesses out there, but how many people are trying to communicate their individuality using the same techniques and phrases. He was taking his bike off its kickstand at this point.

"Explaining to people who you are and what you do simply by using facts is futile. With 328 million voices out there, you're like a raindrop that wants to stand out from the cloud by telling you he's pear-shaped!

"I'll show you. Here's what I do: 'I am logistics and production director, on secondment to Europe from the corporate headquarters of a Fortune 500 corporation. I head up the overseas technology-analysis division, transforming unstructured content data into marketable intelligence units in support of consumer JIT order and fulfilment. *Wake up, dude! You're falling asleep!*"

At this point, I was doubled over with laughter. He was doing this impersonation of Really Boring Corporate Guy, the guy you don't want to get cornered by on a coffee break at a conference.

> "So do you remember what I do? Do you even want to remember meeting me, or would you rather go and swallow half a bottle of bourbon just to erase the memory of ever meeting me? It may hurt to realise it, but nobody cares *what* you do!"

As if on cue, I heard the rumble of engines approaching and four other bikes appeared around the corner. They were twenty minutes late, but it had been an excellent twenty minutes. Over the growing thunder of arriving hawgs, Jack closed by saying:

> "Instead of puking your 'unique selling proposition' all over the poor prospect, treat them like a friend. Tell them something that might interest them."

Very soon there were six hawgs lined up, each headlamp like a Cyclops admiring the view. One by one, the engines switched off and the silence that replaced it was so evident I can only describe it as 'loud.' There was much apology for their lateness. Cormac had had a flat tyre about five miles back down the road, and the others had stopped to help him out. The joys of biking.

Personally, I was ready to head off on the motorcycle and do some quality thinking, reflecting on everything we'd been talking about, but of course we hung out while the other guys let the blood flow back into their legs. There was coffee, a couple of cigarettes for those who smoked, a few locker-room-type gags, and a whole heap of teenage excitement. It was going to be a good few days. By noon, we were ready to get back on the road. Jack mounted his bike and held his helmet above his head. Before putting it on he looked over at me with a deadpan expression.

"Hey, Seb," he said.

"Yeah?"

"This is where you leave the shit behind. Right here!"

Helmets on. Stands up. Throttles back. Minds free.

BORN TO BE MILD

A good story is more effective than a bad argument.

There's a place where myth, legend, and fantasy meet. And, when they do meet, I'd say they have a good laugh:

Legend: Hey, Myth, what ya havin?

Myth: Mine's a cold one, thank you kindly. Have you seen those bikers heading up the pass? A bunch of wage slaves making like they're kings of the road? And they find *me* hard to believe!

Legend: Tell me about it. Reckon they believe having that super-smooth, high-tech, high-price engineering between their knees connects them to salt-of-the-earth, blue-collar, American manhood.

Fantasy: The way they sit on those hawgs, you'd think they all have butt-length hair streaming out behind them, but thems that ain't bald are corporate close-cut. (sings) *Born to be miiiiild!*

I've no problem with that. I know what I'm doing—I'm living a story. Every guy who goes to the golf course on a Saturday morning scrunches up his eyes at least twice during the game and imagines he's Rory McIlroy or Tiger Woods. Have you ever dabbled on Wall Street—five grand on a tip your brother-in-law gave you? Don't tell me you didn't go to bed that night imagining that you were going to wake up as Warren Buffet.

It's all about the stories we tell ourselves.

Some stories are about the place we're headed. Some stories are to distract our minds from unpleasant thoughts. And some stories are about R & R. About getting out and rewriting your dreams and restoring your batteries. That's what my Harley is all about. No, I don't have butt-length hair to let fly in the breeze, but I do have hair, though it's cut short because I work for "The Man."—which limits the potential for heavy displays of hair.

By the time we had mounted up and ridden out, there were about five hours of daylight left. While all of us were happy enough riding in the dark, we didn't see the point of driving through such remarkable landscapes without being able to see them. With that in mind, we reckoned on stopping at a hotel up in the hills.

I can only speak for male bikers but it's no accident that so many guys are drawn to motorcycles. We have the camaraderie of one another's company without the conversation. We're sharing an experience we can revisit through talk at any time we'd like, but as we glide through the countryside, nothing needs to be said. Moving as a pack, we have all the benefits and reassurance that company offers without any pressures, demands, or opportunities to upset one another. For me, it doesn't get more perfect than this. My mind is like a library: thoughts get checked out, new thoughts arrive, old thoughts come back with new twists. If I don't get time to sort out those thoughts and put them on the appropriate shelves, I get agitated, confused, and disorganised. It took about five years of marriage for my wife and me to reach an understanding on this. No matter what time of the evening she went to bed, I found myself staying up an hour later. I didn't even notice the pattern until she started hinting that she thought I was having an illicit late-night affair via the phone or email. Now I will always find a time during the evening to chill on my own, whether I read, watch TV, or catch up on work.

In that regard, I was very happy to be on my motorcycle again. My conversation with Jack hadn't been very long in the grand scheme of things, but there had been a lot of "thought traffic." My mind's librarian had a lot of running around to do, applying the full rigours of the Dewey decimal system to my chaotic thinking. And the remarkable thing was that they weren't all new ideas or thoughts. A great many of the things going around my head were ideas I'd taken for granted: thoughts, notions, memories, and events I'd left to gather dust in the recesses of my mind. These were now resurfacing as paints on an artist's palette for me to illustrate my stories.

I was conflicted, but in a good way. I was enjoying the ride, relishing the company, and playing my part, but at the same time, I was eager to be back at my desk planning my next move. What a remarkable transformation! Four and a half hours before, I had ridden out of my driveway with a nagging feeling in my gut dragging me down. Now the sinking feeling had risen up to my chest and had me raring to go.

Attitude is such a powerful thing. I can see why military people set such store by morale and why governments invest so much in propaganda. When we feel positive and confident, we feel empowered, and that feeling generates possibilities. In a group dynamic, this can become a potent and dangerous force, for isn't that how despots and dictators get a grip over societies—by creating a sense of entitlement, superiority, and confidence within a group? But for me—as an individual 'in sales'—this sense of controlled euphoria was hurting no one, and I felt certain it was going to help me convince my biggest-ever prospect that I was the answer to all of his problems.

What was that about despots and dictators?

And the funny thing is, the boilers that fire Morale and Propaganda are stoked with premium-grade stories: true, fabricated, accurate, or exaggerated.

My thoughts were going faster than the bike when I saw a hand signal coming down the line from Cormac, who was at the front and slowing down. We were a lot higher now. The valley seemed to have narrowed, with denser forest lining either side the road, obscuring the view. My guess was that if the trees weren't there, we would have a fantastic view of the hills.

One by one, the row of handsome Harleys took their places in line, and each of us dismounted. I always get a laugh out of the sense of order we bikers have—after all, we're supposed to be *rebels*. But there's never any concern that the bikes will be parked haphazardly. We always instinctively pull up parallel to the last bike that parked, creating a perfect line.

Helmets off. Heads scratched. Coffee flasks out. Limbs stretched. Cigarettes lit.

Cormac spoke.

> "Guys, I think we took a wrong fork back there. We've covered about thirty miles, and we should have passed through a village by now. I haven't seen anything."

While there might not have been an outburst of panic, a murmur and mutter began across the group as everyone proposed and debated his own theory as to where we were, where we should be, and how to reconcile the two. We had an hour more of daylight, which would be fine if we were on the right road. In fact, even if it were getting dark, we would be OK on the right road. The problem was that if we were on the wrong road, we had no idea where it would take us. And I was not about to blow my cover by announcing that I had a satnav, as I would never hear the end of it. The use of such devices is frowned upon by the club—and many others like it—as map reading and navigation are among the few ways we fair-weather bikers stay in touch with the "old ways." As one guy said to me:

"If you're going to have one of those things, you might as well get an autopilot and sleep your way through the journey."

The club has appointees who look after scheduling, membership, regulation, and overheads, but on the road, other than appointing a road captain to ride out front and set the pace, we try to avoid any form of command structure or leadership. The rationale is that most of us are working stiffs who spend our 9 a.m. to p.m.-whenever slotted into command structures, reporting chains, teams, and groups. As part of our illusion—or perhaps delusion—of being road warriors, we make all decisions collectively. It can be interesting. When you get five guys who are used to doing what they're told trying to make a decision, it can be a bit chaotic, and—with night approaching—a little frayed around the edges. My approach is usually to hold back at first and listen to what everyone else says. If I hear a plan I like, I support it; sometimes, I'll weigh in and put my own plan forward. This time, however, there was something different. I listened to the macho "Let's keep going," the cautious "Let's retrace our steps," and the appeasing "Maybe two of us could go back and check the crossroads." As I listened, I sensed company—I wasn't the only one taking United Nations observer's role in the debate. Jack was down on one knee pretending to fine-tune some element of his perfectly maintained Harley. He stood up, hiked his chaps up, tucked his shirt under the buckle, and gave a short laugh.

"This reminds me of a hiking trip that left from my hometown when I was a kid. I grew up in Colorado, mountains everywhere. Six guys went hill walking and lost the trail. You guessed it—a mist came down. Let's face it, when you can't find the trail anyway, the mist isn't going to make a huge difference.

"Anyways, they were found by a search party two days later. One guy had lost a finger to frostbite, two guys had hypothermia, another guy was dehydrated, one had a bear scratch—and all six were exhausted.

"It turns out they couldn't agree on a course of action, so when it got dark, they hunkered down and stayed where they were.

"They'd all read their mountain manuals, which clearly told them what to do, but they had other ideas."

The list of ailments resulting from the hikers' argument didn't appeal to any of us, and more than one of us looked up nervously at the descending sun. Cormac spoke first.

"So what did the mountain manual say they should do?"

"You do the only thing you're certain will work," Jack replied.

Cormac didn't have time for riddles and games. He simply asked, "Which is?"

"In their case, they could be certain that if they found a stream— even in the mist they could hear a stream—they could follow it down the hill and eventually reach safety. In our case, we can be certain that there's a hotel a couple of hours that way."

He pointed in the direction from which we had come. There was a certain amount of reluctant nodding, and then Shaun chimed in.

"So, if we backtrack and find we've taken a wrong turn, we can go on as we intended. If not, we know we have somewhere we can stay."

The nodding became more positive now. Shaun had highlighted the fact that there was still a gamble, a bit of reckoning, and an adventure. It wasn't an all-out retreat. I smiled at Jack as he straddled his bike. He looked back at me, shrugged his shoulders, and winked.

As we rode out, we were all very focused on where we might have taken a wrong turn. Not that there were many turns. The road clung to the side of the valley all the way with only occasional tracks off it indicating either remote properties or, more often, logging trails. I now realised that we were rising up the side of the valley and that we had actually descended quite deep into it. This suggested to me that we had taken a sidetrack instead of the correct route. Then, with the sun literally sitting on top of a mountain to the west, we came to a Y junction. Sure enough, at this point both roads appeared to be of the same quality and importance. It was an easy mistake to have made.

Cormac and Shaun celebrated with loud revs on the throttle. Within half an hour, we could see the lights of a village in the distance down the valley. In the dusk they were simply a collection of different colours and intensities, but I could map the town out like a multicoloured dot-to-dot puzzle. I could isolate a bar, a fast-food joint, a gas station, a convenience store, a church and—most importantly—the hotel. It was all evident from the position, shape, power, and colour of the bulbs.

In a matter of minutes, we were pulling up outside the hotel. Even though we were all very tired and weary, we still managed to line up our Harleys parallel to one another at the same jaunty angle to the kerb. The plan was a brief and simple one. Get keys from reception, get gear to rooms, get showered, get beer, and get steak. As men with a mission, it was a matter of pride to turn this process around in twenty minutes. The inner child inside each of us was secretly saying:

"Last one down is a loser!"

I could describe the bar to you, but you've seen it a thousand times—if not in person, then in the movies. I don't have to describe the beer to you, either; I'm sure you've been tired and thirsty and know how good it is to slake that thirst with a cold one. One thing I couldn't describe to you is the steak. It was unbelievable. The fresh air and the long day had made me hungry, and I had been concentrating so hard all day that I hadn't thought about food since the sandwich I'd eaten eight hours earlier. I wasn't alone, either. We ate in almost monastic silence and barely a word was spoken until plates were cleaned and second beers were ordered all round.

It must have been about eight in the evening at this point, and regardless of our regular, day-to-day body clocks, we were now synchronised with one another. At this time on a normal workday, Antonio would only be start-ing the busy part of his evening as a chef. Cormac would be having a cup of coffee while taking a pause to reassure the tachometer in his truck that he wasn't driving illegal hours. I can't speak for Alan or Jack, but I usually turn in around midnight. Tonight, however, we would rally for about an hour, then, one-by-one, we would fold soon after 9 p.m. After a brief dis-cussion about the ride so far, conversation inevitably fell to the following day's run.

The route we were following was designed to keep us in the mountains as much as possible. It isn't the world's largest mountain range but it is incredibly beautiful, with hidden lakes, dramatic glens, and wooded val-leys. If we were to simply ride as the crow flies we'd be through them in an afternoon, but our route meandered through the range so as to take in the best of it. The debate now was about the weather. The forecast was for clouds, rain, fog, mist, and the whole nine yards, which would completely cancel out the benefit of the amazing views. At first, as we talked it was all, "Hey, it's bad luck but that's the way things go." Gradually, however, the mood shifted, and some were for changing the route. Antonio had his iPad out and was demonstrating how localised the bad weather was.

> "The clouds are low and they've got caught on the mountains. Over here by the coast, it's gonna be all blue skies."

Cormac was all for staying with the plan.

> "Weather is part of the experience for me, man. That's why I invest-ed in all of that gear. Some of the best views in this kind of terrain are when there's a mist."

It was then that practical Alan reminded us that tomorrow night we weren't going to have the hot showers, tender steaks, and waitress service.

> "Lest we forget, gentlemen, tomorrow night is 'Iron John' night."

'Iron John' nights were what we jokingly called our camp-out nights. If a ride-out was a couple of nights, we usually tried to tie in a suitable outdoor camping location. It was easy to see, looking around the table, that the notion of sleeping out under canvas in the sort of weather we'd been reading about online sort of took some of the shine out of the romantic mists.

Jack had been quiet. Maybe I've seen too many movies, but I didn't imagine he'd have a problem camping out. In fact, I could imagine him hunkered up under an oilcloth drinking tar-black coffee from a billycan while he pared off slices of beef jerky with his bowie knife. Cormac was into it too, and I could see why. He might spend a lot of the time on the road, but it's all in the cab of his Volvo truck, which might be luxurious for a truck, but it's still a bit like living on a space station. This was his chance to breathe in the open air. Alan hadn't spoken either, but it wasn't hard to see that he was more in agreement with Antonio. I guessed that the uncomfortable sensation I was getting around my upper thighs and butt was the fence upon which I was metaphorically sitting.

I like my comforts, but I didn't buy into this whole bike thing for comforts. Far from it. In fact I think I bought a Harley so that when I went out on it, it would remind me how lucky I am to have a warm, comfortable home and a warm, comfortable bed to go with it. The more I thought about it, the less I cared about getting drenched tomorrow night and coming home soaked through to the skin, stinking of wood smoke, sweat, and oil. That being said, I did not want to upset the dynamic of the group. Pistols were not being drawn or anything, but I could see that people could get entrenched in their positions. And the last thing I wanted to report back at the next chapter meeting was that the Mountain Ride-Out split into two groups, or worse, got into a fight at one of the few hotels along the route that welcomes bikers with open arms.

The only answer to the dilemma was to focus on the things that we all wanted out of our bikes in general and the trip in particular. Of course we all wanted different things, but there had to be an overlap. I took a stab at it.

"I have two uncles who are twins, Bruce and Ciaran, and apart from their birthdate, they could hardly be more different. They're a good bit younger than my mother, so they were in their teens during the 1960s. Ciaran bought into the whole hippy thing, but all Bruce wanted to do was become an accountant.

"Anyway, when they left school—I think it was in 1970—a relative in Australia offered them a job in his factory in Melbourne. These days we all know people who've done the Australia thing, but back then it was unheard of.

"Anyway, Bruce was all tied up with his accountancy plans and getting things in order for college upon their return. Ciaran, on the other hand, spent hours in his bedroom, under the Che Guevara poster, reading as much as he could about the hippy trail. Essentially it was the old Silk Road that ran from Europe through Persia, Afghanistan, Pakistan, India, Thailand, and China. At the time, thousands of long-haired, dope-smoking Europeans were making the trek, some in Volkswagen minibuses, some on foot, and others on the growing Magic Bus network. This was how Ciaran planned to get to Australia. He was going to take two months, two T-shirts, two pairs of Levi's, a passport, a copy of *The Prophet* by Kahlil Gibran, and a few telephone numbers.

"Bruce told him he was an idiot. His parents pleaded with him. His friends said helpful things like, 'Cool, man' and 'Right on.'

"I'll cut a long story short. Three months later, Ciaran arrived in Melbourne thirty-five pounds lighter and hollow-cheeked, with scars from Thai police truncheons and a shake in his hands that he has to this day—rumoured to be something to do with malaria, though his father always blamed it on drugs.

"Bruce had flown BOAC, British Overseas Airways Corporation—now known as British Airways. His journey had taken him two days. Every time Ciaran talks about his travels—and it doesn't take much to get him talking—he tells a story I haven't heard before. I have always envied him that journey—obviously not because of the malaria or the truncheons, but because he went through with it. He didn't leave his dream undreamt or unlived.

"And do you know what else? I'm not the only one who envies him. Bruce has confessed to me that even he, the conservative guy, wished he'd gone out and had an experience like that to measure the rest of his life's experiences by."

I didn't actually say anything more. I just kind of left it there. It was a strange feeling, but glancing up I could see they had all been listening.

Alan and Antonio began looking at the iPad again. It turned out that the more closely they looked at tomorrow's forecast, the less certain the blue skies along the coast were. In fact, the prospects appeared to be good for sunny spells on inland, hilly areas in late afternoon!

Cormac had been listening hard to the story. I think he was a little puzzled by its appearance in our conversation, but he had obviously been engaged by it.

"I had an uncle who was at the first Woodstock," he said. "Hair down to his arse in the photos, and according to my aunt, he didn't have a bath during the whole Nixon administration. Hard to believe it now, but he's a market analyst on the London Stock Exchange."

"Hey, Cormac," Jack chimed in, "I guess he's still a counterculture, hippy rebel. If he's a market analyst, he just broke the system down from the inside!"

We had a good laugh. All of us had been beaten up by the crashes of 2008. Pensions, investments, and a fair few hopes and dreams had been left severely compromised. The idea that it had all been a hippy conspiracy was somehow more comforting than the idea that a whole bunch of so-called professionals had actually led us into it.

The nine o'clock lull of which I spoke came thick and fast. We still had no spoken consensus on tomorrow's manoeuvres, but it certainly appeared as if we were tending towards the idea of staying with the plan. Jack had enjoyed watching me toy with his techniques, and I think he was impressed. The key thing for me was that I finally understood the importance of taking the argument out of one context and putting it into another. Once the argument is removed from the distractions of personal, incidental, or irrelevant details, it can be seen on its own merits.

As we walked out of the restaurant towards the rooms, I fell into stride beside him.

Well, how did I do?" I asked.

> "I'll be honest," he replied. "I didn't know where you were going with that one to begin with. In a business context it would have been a bit tenuous, but the fact that we were all guys around a table drinking beer meant it was a story. Guys like stories, what can I say?

> "Then I saw you come in for the kill: the uncle with the shaky hands who had the stories because he'd lived the life. That was good. Real good."

He paused.

> "And what was that bit…'He didn't leave his dream undreamt or unlived.' Oh man, there wasn't a dry eye left in the house!"

That felt good. It felt great to have my mentor praise me, especially when he'd shown himself to be quite reserved. I should have left it at that, but I didn't.

> "I have a few dreams I'd rather not leave undreamt myself," I said, "I'll see you tomorrow."

He winked, smiled, and walked off to his room.

60

WARM BUTTER AND BIG CHEESE

Stories begin with 'Once upon a time' because you seldom get a second chance."

I can confidently say I looked like a lobster ready for the plate. This, however, was an informed guess, as the condensation on the bathroom mirror was about an inch thick when I stepped out of the hottest shower a man could stand.

And the lobster analogy doesn't end with my red, puffy post-shower skin. If you had seen me step into that shower twenty minutes before, you would have seen the bluish tones of a lobster in the wild. Yes, friends and neighbours, for all my heroic talk about my Uncle Ciaran's experiences on the hippy trail, I had led my comrades into the jaws of a serious storm with horizontal hail that put my power shower to shame. It had taken us seven hours to do a four-hour journey. We arrived at the proposed camping ground at what would have been sunset, had we been able to see the sun. The only good thing was that it was already raining, which allowed us to see that the place we would have pitched our tents was very prone to flooding. As a result, we had to put the tents up on an incline. I was sharing with Jack, who had the presence of mind to place the tent with the opening facing downhill. This gave two advantages. One, the opening was sheltered. Two, we woke up where we had gone to sleep. The others had put their tents lengthways across the slope and had rolled into a big heap on top of one another. Our first sight looking out of the tent the next morning was their twisted bodies wrapped in wet canvas, looking like a badly packed pound of link sausages.

Any fantasies about billycan coffee and bacon cooked in the smoke of cedar twigs had washed away with the flood. The storm had calmed down, but it was still drizzling enough to ensure we would not dry out before day's end. With silent, military efficiency we broke camp, wringing out as much of the damp as we could before stowing our goods in our panniers, tank bags, and backpacks. I had braced myself for harsh words from the others, thinking they'd accuse me of encouraging them to continue this route despite the weather. When we got to the nearest coffee shop to thaw out and have breakfast, I was expecting Antonio to pull out his iPad to show me pictures of yesterday's sunbaked beaches along the coast. But it didn't happen. As the coffee infused into our systems and the bacon and eggs went to work, we began laughing and joking with what can only be described as gallows humour.

The Uncle Ciaran factor was alive and well. Alan's description of waking up to find Antonio's face pressed against his ear and Cormac's arm around him had us all breaking our sides with laughter. Antonio imagined trying to describe the scene to his mother, who had never stepped beyond the city limits of Florence. Between the hand gestures, the Italian expressions, and his genuine storytelling powers, we were all doubled up.

Bravely, we paid the bill, stepped from the cosy table in the warm coffee house, and walked out into the grey drizzle, steam rising from our wet leathers. The remainder of the ride was more pleasant than you would imagine, zipped up in a soggy suit, riding through constant drizzle past countless cloud-covered beauty spots. We had a stop for lunch around 1:30, a debrief at the highway truck stop at 4 p.m., and then it was each to his own separate way.

62

I was simultaneously exhilarated and exhausted. The weekend had been everything I wanted from my Harley—and then some. After my first conversation with Jack, my thoughts had all been about work and how I could apply these new concepts to my way of selling. As I coasted through the Sunday drizzle, my biking thoughts and my salesman thoughts began to merge into a cocktail of metaphor, fable, personality types, character traits, business targets, and prospect soft spots. And it was a strong cocktail.

Too often in business, we try to homogenize ourselves, our colleagues, our competitors, and our customers. We break it down to making sales, reaching targets, playing golf, and watching football—all at the expense of the actual personalities we're dealing with. Sure, in sales school we learned to understand people's enthusiasms, challenges, and fears, but only as a way of getting around their defences. I now had the beginnings of a toolkit that would enable me to work with their hopes and fears by talking directly to those emotions and the person who owns them.

I was home soon after 4 p.m., but it was 8:30 p.m. by the time I went upstairs. With the big meeting coming up tomorrow, I should have either gone to my desk to prepare or gone to bed to sleep off the ache of a rather stiff lower back. But I knew that wouldn't be fair to my family, who could have eaten dinner an hour and a half earlier but had waited to hear the salty tales of their road-warrior husband and father. It had been on a Sunday evening like this, after crawling into bed around 8 p.m., that my beloved wife suggested that perhaps she would see more of me if I had opted for the mistress over the Harley-Davidson. Her point was well made and, rather than calling her bluff, I'd elected to make the effort to reintegrate with the family properly after my boys' weekends.

Just as the steaks had revived us all on Friday night, my wife's wonderful cooking stoked my boiler and gave me a big enough burst of energy to carry me through to about 10 p.m. I had enough energy to recount the episode with the three guys in the tent, rolled one on top of the other. I described Antonio's animated storytelling. I described my first encounter with Jack's disembodied voice from atop the rock. Whatever way I managed to describe him, my eldest named him Clint Eastwood, and to this day, any reference to Jack in our household is done under the pseudonym of Clint. It was a great evening, and we all laughed a lot, but by ten o'clock my head felt like a meteor. It was going to hit—the only question was where. I made my apologies, brushed my teeth, and went to bed.

Naturally, as soon as I got under the covers I was wide awake, with tomorrow's meeting running through my mind like a pack of wild mustangs. I was to meet them at 11 a.m. This was the meeting that would clinch the deal. Make or break.

The head of IT had assured me that the CEO was going to be there. This was key. He wouldn't be interested in the product details, those were for the other guys. He was going to have to be comfortable with *me*. And in his eyes, I'm the little guy. It wouldn't matter if I could prove that our systems and processes turned straw into gold; if he had any doubts about this little guy's ability to deliver, he'd order his people to be safe and hide behind the scale and track record of the known, big guy—even if the offering was demonstrably inferior.

Why did I have to start thinking all of this just as I was trying to go to sleep?

I went through the slide presentation in my head. There were thirty-five slides in all. If you were to call one out to me, I could tell you what was on the slide before it and the one after it. I don't leave anything to chance. The slides are for them to look at, not me; my job is to project my conviction and my rock-solid dependability.

If I could answer two questions, I could reassure myself I was prepared and thus be able to fall asleep: *What am I trying to achieve?* and *What has changed since I switched off my MacBook last Friday morning?*

On Friday, I would have said:

> "I'm trying to make a sale by convincing the CEO of my rock-solid dependability."

I've already got the thumbs up from the head of finance on the numbers, and the IT guys have given me the technical all-clear.

On Friday, my anxiety was caused by the feeling that I might not do a good enough sales presentation. So the reality was, I had to sell myself on my own ability to do the job before I could expect someone else to buy my services.

Now I'm totally convinced I'm up to the task. And I'm not just convinced that I, Seb, can do it; I'm convinced that I, *the little guy*, can do it. I could go in and try to sell them all on a product and, if I succeed, possibly generate a one-off sale based on facts, figures, and data that could change tomorrow. But I wasn't going to do that. I was going in there to sell Seb (and whatever company he might choose to represent) as the person to trust, to listen to, and to buy from.

This was my light-bulb moment. Believe me, when you're lying in bed in the dark trying to get to sleep, a light bulb—real or metaphorical—is the last thing you need. My eyes opened wide as headlamps as I realised where logic was taking me, which was to the fact that no slide presentation in the world was going to convince tomorrow's three wise men to make me their Mr. Go-To-Guy. That was a job I had to do myself—man-to-man, face-to-face, eye-to-eye.

Was I going to do it by turning into a talking brochure?

No, I wasn't.

Was I going to do it by delivering a dog-and-pony show?

No, I wasn't.

That just left one thing. I was going to have to tell them a story or two.

I kicked myself under the covers. All that dream time on the bike over the previous two days would have been perfect for choosing, remembering, or even creating the right story to win the day, but all I did was daydream. Yes, I had done the right kind of thinking; I had explored the idea of removing the message from the real context and placing it into a carefully honed story context, so I guess it wasn't so bad. That being said, I still had to identify a story and tell it in what was, for me, a make-or-break situation. And this was my first time using the technique.

I grappled with some of the other comforting clichés I keep in my mental notebook: *If in doubt, tell the truth; Talk about what you know;* and *Keep it simple, stupid.*

I must have talked myself to sleep, because the next thing I remember is a kiss on the head and the click of my light being switched off as my wife got into bed. She later told me that I'd been muttering in my sleep and all she could make out were the words, "bedtime story." I decided to live with the embarrassment because trying to explain would only have made things worse.

I woke up at 6:30 the next morning after the sort of sleep that could only be described as "cryogenic"—the sleep space crews in movies like *Alien* have as they cross galaxies and time warps. If you had told me, as my eyes opened, that I had awoken in the twenty-third century and frogs now controlled the world, I could well have believed you.

As it dawned on me what the day held in store for me, I felt the excitement rise up into my chest and then recede, leaving me with a sense of well-being. I went downstairs, put on the coffee, and put together a bowl of cereal. I always come down an hour before anyone else in the house because I treasure the solitude at that time of the day. By the time they come down I'm ready for them, though perhaps I'm a bit too bright and breezy for their liking.

I ate my cereal looking out the window and listening to the birds. We are fortunate enough to live in what is, for me, the most beautiful corner of the world. Almost instinctively, I reached for the telephone message book on the counter and a pen and began doodling.

What did I want them to feel?

How did I want them to respond?

What did I want them to commit to?

Today was all about emotional commitment rather than signing on the dotted line. In a way, I prefer the dotted-line conversations because at the end of them it's clear-cut—you've either lost or you've won. Today, I had to crank their motors so that they kept idling and revving until we engaged the gears with contracts and steam ahead. There's a delicate balance between being the overeager counsellor, the drinking buddy, or the diplomat. Yes, you have to show conviction; yes, you have to be engagingly friendly; but, at the same time, you have to be dignified and avoid being overly familiar.

It's a situation I've been in many times before with a good deal of success. One reason for my good success rate is that I'm never complacent. No matter how experienced you are, each situation is new; no matter how good you are, you can still be better; plus, on this occasion, I would be introducing a new technique.

I remember the death-row feeling I used to have in my early days as I rehearsed before important presentations. Even with small-ticket prospects, I used to feel like the company's future was on my shoulders, which would lead to negative thinking. Then there would be the meetings that went so well you thought you were a shoo-in, only to get the call the next morning:

> "The board wants to widen the scope of the project. We're going to have to push it out a few months."

Oh boy, those were bad ones. It didn't matter what the reason was—alien abduction, hostile takeover, or leveraged buyout—it always seemed as if it was your inadequacy as a salesperson that lost the business.

Over the years I've learned to focus on all the positives and remind myself why I'm there in the first place. One of the most valuable techniques I have—it sounds a bit crazy at first, but it makes sense—is to tell myself that I am financially independent and I don't need this deal. I've found that, by adopting this mindset, I relax more and care less. Instead of living with the burden of the whole company's future, and that of its workforce, on my shoulders, I become a gentleman of means indulging in some sport.

The cliché we have all been challenging for the last fifty-plus years is:

"Nobody ever got fired for buying IBM."

The first challenge I had in my upcoming meeting was to transfer the confidence the client had in a giant multinational over to my company—but it's more than confidence. The key thing was for me to leave them with the feeling that going *elsewhere* would be the risk. Regardless of whether my company is small and local or global and enormous, I had to leave them with the feeling that the other guys would either be a risk or an experiment, and their business was too important for risks or experiments. They needed to work with a certainty: me.

It's a lovely idea. How would I do that?

I wrote down doodles on the phone pad. They came quite quickly.

It wasn't about knocking the other guys down; it wasn't even about building me up and making me look bigger. No, it was about making me appear solid, immovable, and unshakable. Beside a smaller guy, I had to look big and strong, but beside me, the bigger guy had to look shaky, unstable, and top-heavy.

Nor was it about my company. It was about me. In my opinion, the further up the price continuum you go, the more vital the role of the sales guy. The more technology and money involved, the more important the organic element—the grey matter, muscle and bone. I could be cynical and say that the higher the price, the more the guy client-side needs someone to

68

blame if it all goes down the pan, but I think there's deeper psychology at play. The more he is spending, the greater the risk he is taking. The greater he perceives that risk to be, the more certainty he's going to want. And you don't get that certainty or reassurance from a brochure, a website, or a smiling PR person. You get it from people you identify with and trust. That's why people fall back on previous suppliers—because they are the devil they know. If your prospect is doubtful or hesitant about the person they're relying on to deliver, they are going to feel very uncomfortable. So there's nothing sinister about it. These guys just want someone to hold their hand—someone they can trust to guide them through the process. Or maybe they need a partner—to feel part of a team marching towards a beneficial exchange: I get a sum of money that can be spent on anything, and they get a bespoke, highly specialised piece of equipment that has only one application. You have to sympathise with that though, don't you? If the equipment doesn't perform, they are stuck with it, while the money is stuck with me. If I oversell them on the product's capacity to deliver, I'm not going to have a happy customer. I was never one of those "once I've been paid, I'm clear" sales guys. When you oversell, you're just making a rod for your own back.

The CEO in particular, but really all of them, needed to see me as the lead. They needed to believe in me to the point that I became a key factor in their decision. The key to this sale, and any other sales that were to follow it, was having people look to me for answers. That's the only way I could overcome the "nobody ever got fired for buying Big Blue" trap. I know we have a great product, I absolutely believe in it, but we don't have a big name. If I let this sale come down to our company name versus that of a global corporation, it's as good as lost.

I was beginning to feel quite the megalomaniac, to be honest. The nuts in my granola were getting milled by a set of very militant teeth as I scrawled my notes down on the legal pad, beautifully lit by a shaft of morning light coming in from Mother Nature's own garden.

Obviously I wasn't going to express any of these realisations about the relationship I had to create, but that's not the point. These were the realities
around which I had to build my strategy and play my game.

How long she had been staring at me I had no idea. What I do know is that
I jumped out of my skin when I heard my wife say:

"Who's a busy boy, then?"

She has a beautiful smile, and that morning sunlight was doing nothing
to take away from it. She poured me another coffee and went about her
business, respecting the concentrated look on my face. I closed the legal
pad anyway, as I was done for now. The remainder of my rehearsal would
take place in the car. Usually, this involved cranking up Bruce Springsteen
on the iPod and singing along at the top of my voice, the rest of the world
protected from my vocals by BMW's finest safety glass.

"I have kind of a big meeting this morning. I was just getting some
thoughts down," I said.

"I thought there was something eating you on Friday. I hope it
didn't stop you enjoying your weekend?"

She looked genuinely concerned, which was really nice. I sometimes feel
that, like a lot of women, she sees her man as a bit of a little boy and my
biking trips as an indulgence that she tolerates, but now, from her tone of
voice and facial expression, I saw that she genuinely understood the R & R
value the ride-outs had for me. I put her mind at rest.

"Not at all. The opposite in fact," I replied. "I got a huge amount
of thinking done and a lot of things fell into place. I also got a lot
out of talking to that guy Jack."

I grabbed my briefcase and went to make good my appointment with the
Boss for a duet on *Born to Run*.

I pulled out of the driveway. Just under three days ago I had done the same manoeuvre, out the same driveway, on two wheels. It was hard to believe that, just sixty-eight hours previously, I had been thinking about exactly the same meeting I was thinking about now. It was incredible to think how different I felt now. Then I was concerned, worried, and deflated; now I was pumped, enthusiastic, and eager. I'd even go so far as to say I was singing in tune as I came down the on-ramp onto the motorway. It was a forty-five minute drive to the prospect's headquarters, just on the edge of town. I made very good time despite the Monday-morning rush hour, which was swelled by all the weekend breakers and students heading back to college with clean laundry after a weekend of mom's apple pie. I had scoped out the location the week before, a habit I've developed over the years that makes me feel a bit like a stalker or an assassin but at least means I get to meetings at the right time in the right location. The meeting place was at a point just coming into the city, where the highway goes over a railway bridge, which in turn goes over a river. It's like an illustration from a political geography textbook. I pulled into the business park, which was made up of units of varying sizes, some light manufacturing others sizable office buildings. Theirs was the largest by a country mile. I stopped in a visitor's parking space with ten minutes to spare. I decided to play it cool and use the first five to check emails and texts. I had one from my wife that said:

"Good luck, but remember, it's not luck—it's *you!*" and one from Jack, circulated to all the guys, thanking us for a great weekend.

A couple of other emails had come in, which I marked as unread so that I wouldn't forget to respond to them later on. I checked my tie, collar, beard, and fringe in the rear-view mirror. The rest I would leave in the laps of the gods. I was not going to be the guy caught checking the size of his gut in the wing mirror. It's happened, OK?

It's always good to be occupied before a meeting, whether it's singing duets with Bruce Springsteen in the car on the way, making calls from the car in the car park, or checking emails in the foyer. Doubt stalks the hallways outside meetings, looking for gaps and chinks in the armour for it to slip through and wreak havoc. In that regard, I had played my cards right. The only thing that could go wrong was for the prospect to be delayed and to leave me waiting. That does not promote happy thoughts either. You're left wondering whether they are trying to psych you out or whether your competitor has managed to slip a meeting in ahead of you. Thankfully, today this was not going to happen. I could feel it in my adrenalin-rich, steadily pulsing blood. As I signed in at reception and pinned on my visitor's name tag, I weighed whether I should take the cool, sit-and-read-Forbes position or the stand-and-look-busy stance. I didn't have time to decide. A voice behind me said, "Seb!"

The voice was familiar and assured. It wasn't the "Seb?'" of a person who's looking for someone they hadn't met; it was the warm and positive "Seb!" of familiarity and friendliness. You think I overanalyse? Perhaps I do, but I've heard those three letters whispered, shouted, screamed, and sung in a whole lot of different circumstances. I know a good "Seb" from a bad "Seb".

I turned around to see Dominic smiling at me. His hand was outstretched, and when we shook he augmented the gesture with a grip of the elbow. There was a nervous energy about this that suggested either an over-familiarity with me or an anxiety about what he was leading me into. Neither possibility was particularly good. If he were over familiar with me, this would not bode well with his CEO, who would see some kind of golf-cart camaraderie. If he was anxious about the meeting, that could mean a whole heap of things I wasn't going to allow to get under my skin and make me itch.

We strolled over to a glass elevator that scaled the side of the building's inner atrium, which was a large, roofed courtyard surrounded by offices on all sides. As we went up, we could see into office after office, meeting room after meeting room, each inhabited by a different story in the making. The man and woman to my right—were they talking business or discussing an affair? The meeting to my left didn't seem to be going too well, judging by the expression of the man talking. I imagined a movie based on observations made through these office windows. It made me wonder whether our meeting would be observed. Would my impending triumph or defeat be witnessed live on "elevator-vision"?

We came to a hushed pause on what I took to be the top floor. The doors silently parted, and we walked across a corridor and into a small meeting room. Small it might have been, but this was only in regard to its capacity. There were eight button-tufted leather swivel chairs positioned around a mahogany table. Not a veneer, Office Depot table, but the real deal. On the walls were real oil paintings and, though I am no aficionado, I could've probably guessed the name of at least one of the artists. The interior decorators had wisely chosen the side of the building facing away from town for this room. Instead of overlooking apartment blocks, houses, city parks, office parks, and shopping malls, the view was of the overlapping bridges and the countryside. Dominic came and stood beside me at the window.

"Special, isn't it? The old man has this as his special meeting room. This is where deals are made, promotions offered, and firings meted out," he said.

"Is everyone going to be able to make it?" I hopefully enquired.

"Sure. As planned, there will be Karl, myself, and the old man—"

I interrupted him.

"That's not a habit I want to pick up," I said.

"That's you, Karl, and do I call him Mr. Kergan? Or Alfred?"

"Alf will do nicely," came a voice that sent me out of my skin for the second time that morning. "I take it you're Seb? I've heard some good things about you, Seb."

As I turned around to shake his hand, I was reassured by his demeanour that he had not heard the phrase "old man" in our discussion. He was conservatively but expensively dressed. His suit had not come off a peg, and somewhere in a fashionable gentlemen's outfitters, there was a carefully carved model of his foot, ready for the next pair of bespoke shoes to be ordered. The hair hadn't come cheap either, whether we're talking the

73

expensively trimmed original down the sides or the carefully applied plugs on top. Like his moustache, it was a sandy-brown colour.

I leant forward to shake hands.

"Glad to hear it, Alf. A pleasure to meet you in person."

He and Dominic made as if to sit down. On seeing Karl enter the room, I stayed on my feet. I'd met him before. Karl is about five feet eight, with dark piercing eyes, a serious expression, and what I call a might-as-well-go-all-the-way shaved head that some guys do when they see baldness approaching. He doesn't smile. Period.

"Hi, Karl. Great to meet you again."

He nodded and sat down. The hierarchy was implicit from the seating arrangements. Alf sat at the head, Karl to his right, I to his left, and Dominic over the other side beside Karl.

I had hoped Dominic would be a flank man. I had hoped he would be in a position to introduce me and lead the meeting, in so far as anyone can lead with a presence like Alf in the room.

Now I wasn't sure where it was going to start. Dominic is in systems; I had sold him on the software sometime ago. It's a clear sale for him because it cures all of the pains he has, including some the competition can't. He has peers in other companies I've sold to, and they've backed up everything I've said.

Karl is money. I will give credit where it's due—not that credit is something he is likely to extend to anyone. Karl may not smile, but it's his handling of money that has shareholders laughing all the way to the bank. I have sliced and diced the figures with him—the initial investment, the service contract, the upgrades, and the add-ons. I've given him a cost-benefit analysis I had done for another customer, showing how it improved productivity, lowered costs, and streamlined inventory. During this process

I was quite proud of myself. I'd identified what he liked and I gave it to him. He liked seeing costs cut. He liked seeing reduced personnel time. He liked seeing long service intervals. The very fact that today's meeting was happening at all could be put down to the fact that I had convinced Karl. My research indicated that the Managing Director would be the kind of leader who had enough regard for Karl that he would simply sign off on his word—taking Dominic's buy-in as a given. But one glance at the trimmed moustache, handmade shoes, and hair restoration, and I knew I was dealing with an ego that was not in the habit of delegating anything of magnitude.

Some people will tell you that selling is a science; others will argue that it's an art. Without trying to be seen as sitting on the fence, I can see how you can make an argument for either or both. One thing I am certain about is that it starts with chemistry. And, since I was part of the experiment, I was going to cause a reaction. I set the ball rolling.

"Alf, I noticed from your LinkedIn profile that you're a keen photographer. What do you like to shoot?"

He sighed.

"Sadly, I don't get as much time as I would like to contemplate life through the lens, but when I do, it's landscapes."

"Any particular locations you keep going back to?" I asked.

"You can't beat the west of Ireland. Incredible light, rain or shine."

He said this in a dismissive way, as if to say he wouldn't entertain any argument on the subject. Then he reiterated his opinion.

"Absolutely. Rain or shine, colour or black-and-white."

I wasn't intending to argue about it. "Our changeable weather makes for incredible landscape shots. What kind of camera do you use?", I enquired.

"I've had a range of different cameras over the years but I've settled on a Leica as my main system"

This told me something about the man. In the same way that owning a Harley Davidson tells a story about the rider, owning a Leica tells a story tradition, minimalism and hand crafted quality workmanship. Owners who are willing to pay a significant premium for a higher perceived value.

"What do you shoot yourself?"

"I'd like to be spending more time on landscapes but, like you, time is an issue. On the plus side, I do a lot of travel, which gives me plenty of subjects. I wander around foreign cities and snap whatever catches my eye: details on buildings, passers-by, tourists, vendors."

Having achieved what I wanted to achieve, I now wanted to be the one to bring the conversation back to business. At some other time, hopefully, we would have time to compare notes on photography. Now, however, the last thing I needed was to see his well-manicured finger draw back his expensively linked cuff for a glance at his Rolex Oyster.

"Alf," I began. "I wanted an opportunity to meet with you because, to date, our companies haven't done business together. And, were you to decide you'd like to move to the next step, I thought you might want to know more about whom you would be dealing with.

"To that end, I wanted to ask a few questions to ensure we wouldn't make any false assumptions or have any misunderstandings, or, put simply and bluntly, so that neither of us wastes the other's time. Would that be all right?"

"Sure. Fire ahead."

The words were strident and definite, and his tone curious and guarded. He wasn't used to being spoken to like that. I wanted to show enough guts to stand out from the crowd, but not so much that I made myself look too cocky.

"I have just one concern," I said, pausing deliberately, knowing that I had to hit the right tone between vulnerable and assertive.

"Which is?"

"I'm concerned that we spend a lot of time in discussions and evaluations and even though you feel we have a compelling solution, you will feel compelled to take a safer option and stick with the status quo".

I left that statement hanging there to see how he'd respond.

This might seem like a crazy thing to bring up so early in our relationship but if I've learnt one thing about the bombs that exist in most 'big ticket' deals, you're better off lighting the fuse yourself rather that waiting for it to go off at an unexpected moment later. My experience with a well-known manufacturer cell phones, pagers, and walkie-talkies that I sold to years ago still lives with me to this day. While I was working with them, they undertook a huge outsourcing tender for their entire global logistics function.

"Late one evening while talking with Philip, the head of Supply Chain and Logistics at the firm, he told me confidentially that he had made his selection. They weren't well known here, but they were market leader in the Far East and looking to broaden their net.

"This was of interest to me, as I would be working with them. He made a very convincing case for his choice. He asked me to keep it to myself, as negotiations were still going on.

"The fact that he had made his decision in this way meant he was going out on a limb, but what happened next astounded me.

"Two days later, he called me and said there was a change in plan. They were now going with FedEx. When I asked why there had been a change of heart, Philip confided in me again. When informed of the decision, his CEO suggested he was making a career-limiting decision. 'What do you mean?' Philip had asked. 'When something goes wrong,' the CEO replied, 'and a consignment goes missing—which inevitably happens at some point—emotions run high. The first question people will ask is, *Who lost it?* And when they hear about your friends in the Far East, the response will be, *Who the hell are they? Why are we using a company no one's ever heard of?* And it won't be long before they ask, *Who the hell selected them, anyway?*

"And with that, Philip bowed to persuasion and switched to FedEx. He had gone with an option, which—for their situation—wasn't the best, all because of an irrational fear. When I questioned this logic, Philip justified his position, highlighting FedEx's excellent reputation and track record. I will never forget his response when I reminded him of the glowing review he had given to his initial choice of outsource: 'Life's not that simple, Seb. I'm not going to take the hit just to make someone else's life easier.'"

"So, Alf, my concern is that even if you feel we have the best technical and economic fit for you—you'll still back the big guy......."

I could tell Alf had not been spoken to in this way by a potential vendor. I was all the more glad I had laid the groundwork with the photography conversation. After a brief lull, he responded.

"You make a reasonable point, Seb, but you don't get to the corner office without taking a few calculated risks along the way. I'm happy to take a risk if I feel that I'm backing the right horse."

While I didn't see money being put down or odds being offered, Alf was definitely studying form. Things were going as well as I could have hoped. I tried not to let my relief look too obvious.

"Glad to hear you say that. As I said earlier, I prefer to put all my cards on the table. That way, if we do end up working together, we both know where we stand."

"I appreciate your candour, Seb." He said it in a way that made me feel spoken to as an equal, by an equal. I went on.

"It's well documented how you steered this business out of a tailspin and made it the success it is today but progress never stands still. As you look to the future where do you see the key challenges for the business?

"What do you mean?" he responded quickly, with an edge to his voice.

We're focusing on growing staff levels, investing in a greater product range, increased distribution, more R & D, and above all, more return on shareholder investment." He was fidgeting slightly, from impatience rather than nerves.

"Interesting," I went on. "Those aspects you've mentioned reflect salaries, investment, and overhead—apart from shareholder return, but obviously all of them are supposed to contribute to that—but how are you able to reassure yourself which investments or costs are providing the return and which are actually draining resources?"

He wasn't sure whether this was a rhetorical question or one he was required to answer. To fill the gap, he went for the latter.

"Look, I'm not sure where you're taking this, but to answer your question, I have regular, thorough, and consistent reporting from all department heads, each of whom has provided me with convincing evidence of their measuring systems and the technologies used to acquire those measurements."

The body language told me that he had been asked the same question many times before. He was looking for answers and I'll I was doing was posing questions. Where I saw myself steadily building a cogent argument through a series of steps, Alf saw a long-winded series of questions with no apparent destination. I had to think fast. It didn't take me long to think about Jack's wise words. Funny how I had had that in-depth conversation with him about the power of storytelling, but I hadn't had a story to tell Alf. I remembered kicking myself as I tried to sleep the previous night, berating myself for not using the headspace the bike ride had allowed me to think of a story I could use. I don't know where it came from, but I suddenly remembered an incident from my teens that illustrated what I was trying to say. I needed to help Alf see that no matter how good the individual methodologies deployed by his department heads, if they didn't work in unison, they weren't going to work at all. Feeling inwardly self-satisfied, I smiled outwardly. I hoped that it wouldn't be seen as a scathing smile, but there was no time to worry.

"Sorry, Alf, my fault. Let me tell you where I'm going...like Photography, music is a bit of a weakness of mine. Always has been."

I thought I'd give that a bit of a pause. Let them wonder where it was going and how it could be relevant.

"When I was fifteen, I cut every lawn and hedge in our neighbourhood for a year, working weekends and holidays and nights when I could, just to make up the money I needed to get the best stereo system I possibly could.

"Other kids were saving so they could buy a car, but for me it was a stereo. It's funny looking back now, because today you can store and play your whole music collection on a paper clip. Back then a stereo system meant a block of metal boxes—preferably black—with as many buttons as possible at the front and as many wires as possible at the back.

"I had about five hundred CDs at that point. I wanted a tuner amplifier, a CD changer, a cassette deck—remember cassettes, anyone?—and speakers that would challenge the foundations of the family home.

"I love music, as I say. I knew what quality audio sounded like, having spent more time than was healthy for a teenager with my ear pressed against speaker cones. However, I was not technically minded about such things. I didn't know a volt from a watt. I didn't know a jack plug from jack shit.

"As my money accumulated, I began to wonder what actual equipment I would get. Indeed, the money accumulated faster than my knowledge, and I began to listen more and more to what some of my schoolmates were saying. Alf, as I think you would agree, admiring someone's sense of humour, their dress sense, or their more concrete virtues, such sporting prowess or success with girls, should not lead you to assume that they are experts in high-fidelity audio equipment.

"Two thousand five hundred euro is a lot of money for a teenager to have in their possession. As an amount of money to blow on hi-fi equipment it is, I understand in retrospect, a phenomenal sum. I spent that money in a haze of misinformed ignorance. I found myself with an amplifier that blew the speakers on half volume. I was so impressed by the brand name on the CD changer that I forgot they had earned their reputation with vinyl turntables and were notoriously unreliable with laser and digital technology. The cassette player was so sensitive that it jammed at the slightest stiffness in a tape. As I ascended the extremely tight learning curve while watching my investment go down the other way, I came to realise the only decent investment I had made with my €2,500 was the headphones. The rest of the money I had spilled down a drain, inspired by overblown, trendy advertisements in music magazines, school buddies assembling authoritative speeches out of scraps they had overheard from their fathers and uncles, and sales assistants recognising a good home for redundant stock.

"I was stinging then. I was gutted. But I guess €2,500 is a small price to pay for a lesson bigger than any I learned in four years of college. It doesn't matter how valid each individual's opinion is, it's how they can all work together that leads to success or failure. And only the person at the top, with the overview, can see the connection between them all. Someone else's advice is merely reconnaissance to help you, or some other leader, lead.

"I don't know what kind of music you like, but if you were to take a look at my equipment now, you'd see some names you've never heard of and you'll see others that sell out of dime stores. I listened to everything professionals said, but I made sure to gather enough information of my own to put their advice in a context. I chose each piece of equipment myself. And when you listen to my music system, you can tell if the violinist is missing a single horsehair from their bow.

"So I know where you're coming from, Alf. All the hi-fi experts who helped me waste my hard-earned money were telling the truth. But it was their *individual* truths, not an interconnected truth. I have brought my company's system to your attention for just this reason. On top of its many other functions, it connects the various truths—performance, results, investments, achievements—and gives you a real picture of your business."

I couldn't swear to it—we'd have to have an HD recording to rewind slowly—but I am just shy of certain that I saw Karl's eyebrows raise a millimetre and the trace of a smile curl the corner of his mouth.

Whatever happened that caused me to pause, think of Jack, and summon that story to mind—it was close to a miracle. The course I'd been pursuing before that, asking him haughty questions about how he gathered information, would have been the road to ruin. As a salesman I learned long ago that body language is the most eloquent language there is. Alf had gone from the poise of a statesman, to the fidgets of a six-year-old during a long church sermon. Now he was back.

And it wasn't just the change of tack; it was specifically the use of a story that helped me get Alf's attention and respect. And respect does have to be earned. Like trust, and many other attributes, it is the other person who attributes them to you. You can't demand them for yourself.

How different things would have been if I had used a slide presentation with its point-to-point, blow-by-blow information about performance. Alf was biting. Alf was not interested in the product for itself, he was interested in its reliable delivery. No slide presentation was going to convince him that I, Seb, was the man to make that reliable delivery, but the story had. I went on.

> "I'd like you to cast your mind six months forward from now and visualize everything exactly as you want it, working perfectly. What would the difference be between today and that day in the future?"

Alf paused for thought, buying himself some time. "That's a good question, Seb…We would be competing more effectively, and we'd have a more compelling story to tell our investors."

It occurred to me how different his requirements were than those of the IT guys. They would have been talking about integration, risk reduction, scalability, and performance—the details of their domain. Alf was, as indeed any MD should be, a "big-picture" man.

> "Alf," I said. "May I share a concern with you? If you could get those benefits from your existing vendor—which they will claim you can—why would you consider working with a company like ours? From where you're sitting, we are high risk."

"Well," he said, speaking hesitantly for the first time, "to be totally straight with you, Seb, you're right. I hadn't really been taking your company too seriously."

Oh, this was good!

"And now?" I said quietly.

"You have my attention," he said confidently, looking me directly in the eye.

"I wasn't sure you were interested, Alf. What did I miss?" I asked.

"Let's just say your competitors haven't been as responsive as I'd like them to have been," he said in a rather weary tone.

This was an opportunity I was not going to let pass me by.

"And when you told your current supplier that your business was growing and changing, that you need greater responsiveness, what did they say or do?"

"We're still waiting." The weary tone had been joined by gritted teeth.

I had heard what he said. I had understood what he said. But I have found that getting prospects to repeat negative comments about my competition makes the issues they are causing for their businesses more real and present, thereby distinguishing me and highlighting the benefits that I can offer.

"I'm not sure I understand?" I said, looking puzzled.

"They have yet to come up with the goods," he said solemnly.

"And how does that feel?" I probed.

"Let's put it this way: it's why you're here." He was not going to submit to psychoanalysis, that was for sure.

"So, what were you hoping I could do?"

"I'm looking for someone who will take the time to understand my business. I want someone to bring me a solution that works at least as well as he promises it will, that doesn't cost the earth, and that won't be obsolete in eighteen months. It's not a lot to ask."

There was anger in his voice, but my stand-back approach had worked. In getting him to think about his pain—and those who had failed to address it—I was both a confidant and a potential solution provider.

"What else?" I enquired.

"I want a solid assurance that, if we buy from you, you're not going to disappear the moment contracts are signed. That you will be on hand to answer for any shortcomings we may see in the system— and, indeed, to accept any praise that may be due."

He was talking frankly, and though it was the first time I had met the man, I could see he enjoyed the freedom and simplicity of two people speaking their minds.

"About those other priorities, Alf," I said, coming back to the functional side of the issue.

"You said you wanted to compete more effectively and to have a better story to tell your investors. Which one of these is at the top of your priority list?"

"Both are priorities. They're equally important. But competing more effectively is a good story in itself, so I guess that would be the top of my list."

This was fair enough. I pursued this line of thinking.

"And how would you see a system like ours helping you compete?"

"Well, it's no secret that we've fallen behind our competition. We still have a reputation for quality, so I believe fulfillment must be central to the problem. My overriding priority is to not just catch up with but to overleap the market."

This was a very real illustration of why Alf needed to know me and to trust me. This conversation had nothing to do with Dominic's IT issues or Karl's accounting ones. I was having a heart-to-heart with a captain of industry about his personal pains.

"And how does 'falling behind the competition' manifest itself?"

"Depends on whose perspective you take. It's not perceived the same if you're in sales as opposed to finance, for example. Production has a different take on it again."

And there he was, feeding back to me the very point I had made earlier about connectedness. And he was submitting to psychoanalysis after all.

"And which matters most to you as MD?"

"Well, my immediate priority is to halt the slide in sales. If we have product being bought and income coming in, we will have the resources to work on the systems that lie in-between. Falling sales means fewer resources to invest in remedies like those you're offering."

"What sort of a 'slide' are we talking about, comparing last year with this year?"

I used to find it a struggle to ask prospects the tough questions; it felt as if I was poking my nose in their business. But it's essential, as I've learned the hard way. Like a doctor, you're not going to be able to prescribe a cure if you don't get a clear picture of the ailment. If I was going to help him turn things around, I needed to know the scale of the problem. I couldn't make promises or projections without facts.

"Well..."

He knew he was divulging sensitive information, and as he spoke, I could see him deciding to trust me more and more.

"Sales were down 7 percent last quarter on the previous quarter. There are no outside market factors I can blame for it, and I don't see a reversal—unless we can achieve something ourselves."

"Is it not just a seasonal thing? Is there not a bounce in the busy season, when people start buying television and satellite equipment for Christmas?" I said hopefully.

"Seb, you don't understand."

There was a pain in his voice, not aimed at me, but caused by what he was saying.

"Last quarter *was* our busy season. Our biggest customers are retail, and they place their orders two quarters ahead of the market."

"And is the market down, or is the competition stealing your lunch?" I sort of knew the answer to this.

"They're not just stealing our lunch, they're eating right under our noses."

I hadn't realized there was so much of an urgent need within the company. From my conversations with Karl and Dominic, I had seen this as a housekeeping issue: improving systems to keep the company on a successful plane. Now I realized they needed to be lifted out of a hole.

"So what are they doing differently? I'm familiar with their products, and they're not exactly leading edge."

"Imagine you're a buyer for a large retail outlet. You don't want to carry large amounts of inventory. You order little and often, so you have to have absolute confidence in the supplier's ability to deliver on time."

He paused before going on.

"So the retailer tells our salesman that he wants 250 units next Wednesday at 10 a.m. He takes it down and says it will be forty-eight hours before he can confirm shipment."

This seemed a bit nineteenth century to me. I was genuinely puzzled.

"Why doesn't he just call the factory?"

"It's not that simple. He can call the warehouse and check what's in stock, but that brings its own problems."

I was listening. "Such as?"

"Say we only have two hundred units in the warehouse. The sales rep then has to check with the production line to see how long it will be before the remaining fifty units are available."

As he told the story, he was getting older before my very eyes.

"I can see how that might complicate things," I said. In this day and age, that was not a satisfactory situation.

"Now imagine if two sales guys call in and check on the same stock for two different customers?"

"Has that ever happened?" I said, with eyebrows raised.

"More than once," he said wearily.

"So what did you do to fix it?"

"We've installed a log in the warehouse that records all the orders that have been committed and to whom."

"And it's working?"

"It averts disaster but creates its own problems by slowing us down. To play it safe, people reserve stock. We can have product on reserve after a customer has changed their mind and is getting an alternative delivered by our competitor. We're very competitive on price, but our competitor is still outselling us at every turn."

"Even though they're more expensive?" I asked. I knew his products were good quality; it didn't make sense.

"Remember, our guy had to phone up the warehouse and production. The sales guy for the competition just takes out his tablet device, checks availability, and quotes a price and a delivery time there on the spot. Who would you order from?

He looked at me, as if to see whether I was genuinely putting myself in a retailer's shoes.

"So your salespeople are losing deals to their competitors' technology? How's that affecting morale?"

"That's another cause for concern. Two of my best people resigned last month," he said quietly, leaning backwards as if to signal his despair. Again, I heard, but I had him teetering on the brink and I wanted him to jump.

"Sorry?"

"Two of my best salespeople have resigned," he repeated more loudly.

"It's not really an issue you could quantify, is it?"

"It would be difficult," he said pensively.

"Well, imagine we're at the end of your financial year. What revenue would you expect if this issue was fixed?"

"I'd expect to be north of €200 million."

"And if you do nothing?"

"We might get to €180 million."

It wasn't a prospect he relished recounting at a shareholders' meeting.

"And how much of that €20 million goes to the bottom line?"

"At a 35-percent margin, about €7 million."

"Forgive my ignorance, Alf, but is that a little or a lot in your business?"

"The honest answer? It's the difference between staying in business or going out of business."

This was frank talk to be sharing in front of two staff. It must have been something they had already discussed. I went on.

"This might be obvious to you, but I have to ask. Where does fixing this fit into your overall scheme of priorities?"

"It's number one, no question of that."

And from his tone, this was no lie. As he saw it, he was hemorrhaging and needed a tourniquet. It was time to clarify his levels of pain.

"Let's see if I've got this straight. You're losing sales because your salespeople can't be as responsive as their competitors. You're losing key salespeople because they're losing sales and commission—through no fault of their own. And this is costing the business around €7 million over a twelve-month period. Fixing this is your number one priority. Do I have this correct?

"That's it, in a nutshell." He sighed.

He was still the dignified, composed, and perfectly presented gentleman I had seen on my arrival, but the weight of the world was now visible on his shoulders. So I brought him back to life with:

"Should we talk about money now?"

"I should see the proposal first?"

It was half question, half statement.

"There may be no need for a proposal, Alf. When I tell you how much our solution would cost, you'll probably want to call security—if you haven't fallen off your chair first."

This raised a much-needed smile.

"Try me," he said.

With a serious expression on my face, I answered.

"I can't give you a number I can stand over just yet. Having worked on similar-sized projects in this sector with equivalent challenges, such as remote, automated order processing, when you include everything, software, hardware, professional services, training and

support, you're looking at an investment between €3 million and
€4 million."

I paused for effect before adding:

"Should I get my coat?"

"It's a lot of money. An awful lot of money. Certainly more than I
had planned on spending."

He hadn't blown me out of the park. He hadn't even said he wouldn't pay it.
This was merely an expression of surprise, like someone going to the doctor
with a stomachache and being told it's the appendix. I was tempted to start
justifying the price. I then remembered an important lesson I learned from
a colleague, Julia, with whom I had worked at another software company.

Julia was a consistent top performer. She was assigned to me as a mentor,
and I occasionally got to shadow her on sales calls. In eight of the ten years
between 2000 and 2009, she outsold every other salesperson at our Fortune
100 employer. Year after year she was consistently the first rep to make the
company's exclusive "President's Club"—a gathering of elites reserved for
the best of the best.

At one meeting, I witnessed Julia preparing her prospect for price shock.
Before giving them the price of her proposed solution, she said:

"John, I want to make sure you're sitting comfortably, because
when I show you the price I have for you, you're going to fall off
your chair."

She reached across the table and showed him a single piece of paper. The
blood drained from his face while she sat back in her seat opposite him,
relaxed and confident.

As it dawned on John how much it was going to cost to fix the problem
Julia was helping him solve, he began to shift uncomfortably in his chair.

The paper shook in his hand. With his voice raised half an octave higher and trembling slightly, John turned to Julia and demanded:

"How can you justify this price?"

Julia sat quietly, for what was probably only six or seven seconds but seemed like and age, before responding.

"You look shocked," she said nonchalantly.

"It's not just a look," he said. "I am shocked. I mean, it's just so much higher than any of your competitors."

"We usually are," Julia replied comfortably.

"But let me ask you this: Why do you think our customers consistently pay us more?"

I was fascinated by this exchange. I had no idea how John would respond, so I waited anxiously while he pondered Julia's question. Then his answer came.

"Well, I suppose your software is easier to integrate with our existing system, and from what I hear, your support is excellent."

"Is that worth paying more for?" Julia probed.

"I suppose it could be," John responded.

As he answered, John visibly relaxed. The tremble left his hands and his voice returned to its normal, deep pitch. As we returned to Julia's car, I remarked on what I had observed. I drew particular focus to the way Julia had resisted the temptation to become defensive when John questioned her price. I'll never forget her parting remark to me.

"If you just give the prospect ten seconds longer, he'll answer his own objections."

From a psychological perspective, what Julia said to me made perfect sense. A high price creates dissonance in the brain—that uncomfortable feeling that catches the subconscious mind between the fear of paying too much and the excitement that you are buying something special.

In order for the dissonance to dissipate, the brain must decide the reason for the high price: Am I being ripped off or am I buying something special? In order to resolve the dissonance, the subconscious brain will look for clues to help it decide.

The more the seller tries to resolve this dissonance for the prospect, the greater the risk of feeding his fears. We've all found ourselves asking ourselves things like, *Why is this sales person trying so hard?* or *What is he or she trying to hide from me?*

However, if we allow the prospect to resolve his own dissonance, the subconscious will accept his reasoning as fact. People always accept their own data as fact.

Allow the prospect that extra ten seconds of space and time, aided by some gentle, reflective questioning:

- Why do you think it's more expensive?

- Why do our customers pay us more?

- What would you need to get to feel it was worth paying more?

Then settle back and listen to them answer their own questions.

Back at the mahogany boardroom table, there was an awful silence as Alf let it all sink in.

94

"And what do I get for this kind of money?"

"I don't wish to sound smart, Alf, but you get to turn the tables on your competition and start winning again. You get to jumpstart the morale of your sales reps and deliver €200 million to the business,"

I answered coolly and confidently.

"Is there a cheaper way to do it?"

Karl spoke, for the first time since we had sat down.

"There's always a cheaper way Karl", I responded, "but let me tell you what I believe to be true about cheaper. I was in Paris a few months ago attending a conference. I had taken a taxi from Charles de Gaulle Airport to the centre of Paris, which cost me €65. Before it was time to return, I discovered that you could get a train ticket for €8. A train I thought would be faster, more comfortable, and a whole lot cheaper.

"When the conference was over, I checked out of my hotel and made my way to the local metro station, dragging my suitcase past a line of taxis as it started to rain. When I got to the metro station, I purchased my €8 ticket and made my way down two flights of stairs. There I waited and waited and waited until finally the metro arrived and took me three stops to where I was to transfer to the airport metro. The second station was heaving. Everybody seemed to have the same idea. Have you ever tried to get a heavy suitcase through a turnstile designed to allow only one person through at a time?

"Again I had to wait and wait and wait. The Charles de Gaulle train finally came, and I was caught in the crush to board. My case got stuck in the closing doors of the train. Old ladies were jumping up to help me. It was embarrassing.

"After standing the whole way, I arrived at terminal three—only to find my plane was leaving from terminal one. I had to catch one of those magnetic levitation trains to whisk me to terminal one. The escalator was out of order. Tired, cranky, and sweaty, I arrived at the check-in desk, only to be told that my flight had just closed. I would need to stay overnight, as the next flight home would be in the morning. The additional cost? Five hundred euro. This was all because I wanted to save a few euro. I learnt that day that cheap always has a price."

There was a silence. If two employees had submitted receipts for those two journeys—the taxi and the metro—to Karl, the taxi guy would have gotten a talking to for being extravagant. Hearing the story in blow-by-blow form, he couldn't argue with it.

"You are right, of course. If your software does what you say it can do, we'll break even after six months. I can see that. At the commitment stage in the process, it's up to us to believe whomever we award the contract to," said Alf, looking at Karl.

"Alf, when you make an investment of this size, what decision process do you typically go through?"

I now wanted to set my self up for leaping over any other hurdles that might be along the way.

"Because this is not budgeted to this extent, I will need to go to the board to get sign off," Alf said in a serious tone.

It was a bit of a step away from what he had said earlier about being the MD and making the final decisions.

"What barriers do you anticipate?" I asked.

"Not too many. The money is there; I already submitted a business case. I just need a proposal to fill in the details."

96

Alf was sounding ripe and ready. This was a good meeting. Dominic then chimed in.

> "I'd like to run a pilot to make sure you can integrate with our existing systems."

> "That makes sense. Can we do this first? Can we put it on paper first, along with the numbers, and if all that passes muster and the money is made available, then we can proceed to a pilot—how does that sound to you?"

I wasn't going to jump through hoops or involve any of our other people without some form of commitment.

Alf and Dominic looked at each other, Dominic looking for Alf's approval before nodding his assent, allowing me to say:

> "That makes perfect sense. Dominic and I can discuss the details of the pilot at another time."

At this point, the perfectly manicured finger pulled back the exquisitely linked and starched cuff to reveal the Rolex Oyster. Alf checking the time was a sign that he was happy with his decision and he has mentally moved on.

Alf was as intelligent and decisive as he was debonair. These qualities were all part of his role as judge, arbiter, and executor. Dominic would keep the wheels turning in the engine room, Karl would ensure fiscal buoyancy, but, unquestionably, the captain of the ship was Alfred Kergan.

I walked out of the meeting exchanging firm handshakes with all. Alf and I appeared to have made a connection, and Karl stopped briefly to scratch his head before taking a call on his mobile. Dominic looked relieved and reassured as he saw me down to the reception area.

"You did really well there. I've never seen anyone play him like that."

"It was just a matter of getting him to tell me his story, so I could tell him one back with a happy ending. And somehow, it seems to have been the right story."

We agreed to talk the following morning about next steps. I went out to the car. I wasn't in the mood for more Springsteen, so I decided to have a bit of quiet time and think things over. It had gone very well, but not the sort of very well you can predict. And when something starts unpredictably, it can just as easily end unpredictably.

The first guy I ever admired in sales—and there haven't been many—was a guy called Danny. He used to say to me:

"Selling is like spreading butter on fresh bread. If you take the butter straight from the fridge, you're going to make a mess of things. You gotta warm the butter, Seb. You gotta warm the butter!"

On that basis, three good things had happened today:

I'd met the big cheese.

I'd warmed the butter.

I wasn't left crying over spilt milk.

PEACOCKS AND GREAT DANES

First rule of networking: There is no trump in a pack of business cards; it's all in the play.

If I hear either of these statements again, I think I will probably scream:

> "If you're not networking, you're not working," and my favourite,
> "You have to network to get work."

Yes, I know they're true. Without networking and adding links to your social and professional chains, your business will contract rather than grow. In other words, networking bears fruit, and if you don't network, chances are that your business will end up shrivelled like a prune.

Again, I know it's true. It just seems that over the last fifteen years, "networking" has turned into a religion peopled by zealous followers who worship at the altar of the pressing palm, determined to save us all from the damnation of an empty order book. The reality is that I hate networking, especially the organized, big-room variety. I think my discomfort stems from a moment when, as a very young child, I got lost in a large department store. I still have this vivid memory of standing in the drapery section crying, surrounded by all these well-meaning shoppers asking me my name and what my mother looked like. The name of the department store was, ironically:

"The Monster House."

On a visit to New York a couple of years ago, I went into Macy's department store to buy a present for my wife, and the same sense of foreboding washed over me. I turned on my heels and left. It's funny the way childhood experiences—often long since forgotten—can be suddenly triggered, causing us to choke-up decades later.

A friend told me once that I have agoraphobia. Apparently the first part of the term, *agora*, is the Greek word for marketplace. The whole word means "a fear of open or public places." If that's what it means, that's what I've got. Some people would have been afraid in that meeting room on Monday, cowed by the intimidating presence of Alf with his mahogany and leather business suite—I wasn't. But for me, trying to work a hotel function, the room filled with people, servers clinking glasses as they try to balance plates with sandwiches in their other hand, is like trying to slow dance with a tiger in a hammock—awkward, frightening, and ultimately dangerous. That being said, I acknowledge that many times you have to do the uncomfortable to achieve the desirable. In a lot of awkward situations, I set myself targets and rewards. And here was my current plan: get to talk to the two key people I wanted to meet, and then reward myself with an afternoon off. It was Friday, after all.

Anyway, I have assigned networking, like cold calling, to the "you don't have to like it, you just have to do it" category of selling activities.

I think that because I dislike networking so much, in a strange way I've become quite good at it—when I choose to do it. I target an event where I feel I'm likely to bump into people who are of use to me. My wife, who is a natural connector, sees this as quite manipulative, like I'm using people. I see it as practical. Besides, the people who go to these events are not stupid, and they're not going to let me "use them" unless there is something in it for them. It's a win-win.

Once I've identified an event, I try to get the registered list of attendees. This is usually easy when you're a member of the organisation hosting the event. Then I make a shortlist of the people I want to meet. I like to arrive a little late so I can check the registration table. I pretend to be looking for my badge when what I'm actually doing is scanning the table for those on my list. If their badges are still on the table, it means that they are either late or have decided, at the last minute, not to attend. My goal is to whittle the shortlist down and have a meaningful conversation with two people. My reward is to then leave the event to those who have nothing better to do and head home to be with my family. That's the secret to my networking motivation. Arrive late and leave early. Commando operation. Get in, get target, get out.

I have joined a couple of networking groups over the years. I think the problem for me was that they were too general. If I'd been a printer, a florist, or an insurance salesman, people would have understood me and I would have had something to offer them. The little work I got through these channels was either incidental or accidental.

So what was I doing at a Chamber of Commerce function? Had I come to hear the speaker—the first Irishman to swim the Bosphorus in a tuxedo (or some other arcane achievement)? I think not. I had retained my Chamber of Commerce membership because at least it had a significant corporate membership. What I like about the chamber events is that they have some big hitters on their council and there is almost an obligation on these guys to attend, especially the more important events. It makes for an interesting cocktail. You have five to ten industry leaders and perhaps two hundred mom-and-pop operators, from semiretired librarians who have become life coaches to sales reps from the ubiquitous office-supply companies.

My first target was Henrik Laursen, a Danish engineer and CEO of a company that had set up a distribution centre in the city. Laursen was on the Chamber Governing Council. The other was Charles Canterbury, who had recently taken over as CEO of a Canadian company headquartered nearby. These were my sole targets and the only people I wanted to talk to. The trouble is that the strange phenomenon common to all functions, not just networking events, comes into play. You arrive on your own and find yourself standing at the centre of a very large, crowded room—just like the child lost in a department store. As you stand there, you believe you are surveying the scene and gathering your wits, but you are actually bait dangling on a hook. By some natural force yet to be given a scientific name and formula, you are going to attract the person in the room you least need—or want—to talk to. And once engaged in conversation with someone to whom, if given the choice, you would have given a wide berth, you are now faced with the challenge of escaping their clutches.

It appeared as if everybody wanted to talk, and why shouldn't they? They were networking, after all. It looked as if their sole objective was to grab every opportunity to swoop in on their prey—large or small, nutritious or otherwise—and each person had his or her own targets. It's a bit like planes in a holding pattern above a busy airport, which have to keep moving, keep lining up on their target, so as to be ready to move in and land when the opportunity arises. A consistent babble filled the room. With four hundred people in attendance, there were probably 150 separate conversations going on in different pitches, different tones, and on different subjects. Nevertheless, it all became a blanket of sound across the room. As I made my way to the buffet, looking busy as I placed a few chicken skewers on my plate, and then back out into the crowd, I began to discern snippets of voices as I passed. Like broken fragments of pottery made into a mosaic, the sentences all seemed to fit together neatly without making much sense. Pets were mentioned, as well as cars, holidays, children, junior schools, senior schools, universities, growth, fast food, green energy, death, and taxes. You name it—they were all talking about everything but work. Then it dawned on me. They were relating anecdotes and sharing experiences. In other words, they were telling stories.

I don't know why, but this was a surprising realisation for me. I had taken part in these conversations countless times, but I had never stopped to think about it. I knew that networking was never about ramming what you do down someone else's throat, but you have to leave an impression, otherwise why bother going?

"Be interested, not interesting," my old boss used to tell me.

"What if they're just boring old farts?" I used to worry.

And let's face it, who hasn't met their fair share of BOFs at these events?

There is this paradox in selling. The more you try to leave a positive impression, the more likely you are to leave an unfavourable impression. When Betty Babble gets talking with Bernard Bored at a function like this, Betty is hoping to leave a big enough impression on Bernard that he will remember her long after the event has finished. So, perhaps I'd misunderstood the whole networking thing. Maybe it had caused me discomfort because I was being paid to promote my company and its products, yet I was just involved in idle chatter about kids, golf tournaments, and TV shows instead. But people don't connect at the "what have you got" level. They connect at the "who are you really" level. Stories, it seemed, were the best way to manage this crossover.

You live and learn.

And now my opportunity to exchange banal pleasantries with Mr. Laursen had arrived. Despite the fact that he was one of the only two people in the room I actually wanted to speak with, I still had to gather myself so as to avoid being the very person I myself would avoid. Luckily I'm good at homework—it's essential—I knew a fair amount about the man and his company.

We all have an inbuilt faculty to resist unsolicited proposals, suggestions, or advice that is offered to us—even ones that make sense or ones that would yield us profits. We resist either because we've made up our minds already or because we feel under siege. The louder, more persistent, or insistent a person is, the faster our shutters go down. So I could go right up to Mr. Henrik Laursen and tell him something amazing—that my solution could increase his profits or cut his costs—and, whether it's true or not, he'll just perceive me as another needy sales rep.

I had to get him into a position where he was curious to know more about my company and me. If he were curious, his shutter would stay up and the lights on. I had to manoeuvre the conversation to a place where he was asking the questions and I was giving him trimmed-down answers. Simultaneously, I had to get him to buy into me. Like I said, the other 398 people in the room were busy getting lost in the "me too" noise, in the vain hope of generating interest.

As I tried to get my mind into this critical position, I was distracted by the mental image of a National Geographic programme. The male bird of paradise with its feathers erect, broadcasting his talents to potential mates with a display that seemed to say:

> "Look at me—I've got everything you need and the feathers to prove it!"

All this had flashed through my head in the time it took me to make my way down a few short steps to where the momentarily lone Henrik Laursen was now standing.

I had caught him at that perfect moment when he had withdrawn from his previous conversation and was now trying to look purposeful rather than lost or alone—just that moment when you're vulnerable to bores. This meant our encounter could be a casual, ships-passing-in-the-night affair rather than a formal approach, which would have made him raise his defences.

> "Hello, I'm Seb…Henrik." I leant forward slightly, as if to read his badge. He replied cordially, perhaps relieved that I appeared not to know who he was. I noticed he had ducks on his tie. Not Donald or Daffy-type ducks but beautifully embroidered ducks. They were arranged in diagonal lines, which gave them the appearance of birds flying in formation. I hazarded a guess.

104

"Are you a hunter?" His face lit up with a combination of enthusiasm and bafflement that I should know. He nodded in a similarly quizzical way that meant I really had to explain myself.

"I'm sorry. I couldn't help noticing your tie," I said, pointing at his shirt front.

He smiled. I had made a connection. Instead of being a potential sinister stalker, I was an empathetic comedian with, perhaps, a comparable level of passion in my own areas of interest.

"Where do you like to hunt?" I asked, a general enough question, I thought.

"I have only been based here for the last twelve months, and since I am taking over a new position, I have been so busy I haven't had the chance. Normally I am hunting in Denmark and the Frisian Islands."

"That's a shame," I said. "I've been out a few times over the years to shoot clays, but I can't claim to be a hunter. My neighbour is secretary of our local gun club; I'm sure he'd be delighted to take you under his wing—if you'll pardon the pun. We live about half an hour beyond the city, and there are a few good duck marshes around the area. It's a beautiful spot and perfect for mallard hunting. They have all the hides, decoys, and gear you'd ever need. I'm sure they'd let you borrow equipment if you don't have any with you."

As we exchanged business cards, I wondered if I had gone too far. Apart from any social presumption on my part, I wondered if had I crossed the sacred line into my home territory, which I guard fiercely. The look of unrestrained, schoolboy glee on his face told me that, if I had been overly friendly, it was appreciated. He then launched into his findings regarding duck species in the various territories where he had hunted. Apparently there was significant overlap between waders found in Irish waters and those found on the North Sea. I was beginning to get out of my depth, so I decided to bring the conversation back within my control.

> "It's funny we should be talking about birds, because I had a funny thought a few minutes ago. Looking at the people around the room passing cards is like watching one of those nature programmes."

I picked up some momentum.

> "You know, the National Geographic programmes where you see birds—birds of paradise, peacocks, that sort of thing. They fluff up their feathers, they dance, they strut around trying to impress the females, but the females just ignore them."

He had that slightly quizzical look again, but I didn't take it personally. Rather than meaning that he thought I had lost my reason, I realised it was a sort of preliminary smile, a readiness to laugh.

In a strong Danish accent, he said:

> "I know exactly what you mean. The peoples with something to sell are trying to look very cool and calm as they talk about themselves. At the same time, the other people are nodding and smiling very politely, as if they are not really interested."

I was beginning to wonder where this put me. I had inadvertently put myself in a position whereby, if I told him what I did for living, he would immediately see great big feathers sprout from my backside to my shoulders and an ornate crest appear on my forehead. As I was anxiously looking for the reverse gear on my analogy, his shoulders began to heave convulsively with restrained laughter.

> "It's a good thing." He spluttered. "It's a good thing the room is full of peacocks and birds of paradise!"

He paused. As I was genuinely puzzled, I asked what he meant.

106

"Have you seen how ducks mate? We'd all be drowning each other, ha ha ha!"

I'm no expert in birds, and I can't say I've witnessed ducks courting, but I was caught by his enthusiasm and joined in the laughter. He then glanced away to greet someone rapidly approaching us from behind.

A broad-shouldered, conservatively dressed individual approached confidently, but seemed sensitive to the fact that we were in conversation. Henrik greeted him in a manly fashion.

"Charles, my friend, how the hell are you?" he bellowed through a smile that stretched from ear to ear.

"I'm great, Henrik. How are you? Good to see you," he added before waiting for a response.

"I saw your name on the registration list and your badge was missing from the table, so I hoped you'd be here."

"Charles Canterbury, I'd like you to meet Seb."

There I was, in a room filled with four hundred people standing around trying to balance plates, glasses, egos, prospects, hopes, and even dreams. Some of them were talking about their children, their summer holidays, or pretending to ask advice about which car to choose in their trade-in. Others continued pushing their wares, overtly trying to persuade people to take them seriously and boldly thrusting business cards into their hands. As I looked down at them, my eye automatically divided them into strutting, glistening blue-and-green male peacocks on the one hand, strutting in front of bored, disinterested, fidgety, dull-grey females on the other, their voices merging into a background cluck-and-coo.

Despite their bravado and hail-fellow-well-met demeanour, it was clear Henrik and Charles were not all that well acquainted and that my presence was facilitating rather than inhibiting their meeting. I have a great many potential prospects on my hit list and these were the only two that were attending this event. Was it a coincidence I should find myself with standing with the two of them? Luck? Good fortune? Or good planning. Within the swathe of businesses represented by the throng, these guys were very much in the minority: ex-pats, head of multi-national outposts, both there as much out of diplomacy and public relations, as they were in a commercial role. The reality was, people like that probably gravitate toward one another out of affinity and empathy.

For the most part, we talked about the state of business in general and in our three respective countries. Though both of them came from countries that spent significant periods of the year under snow, they agreed that Ireland's continual rain was depressing. In defence, I suggested that Charles Canterbury could not hail from the Maritime Provinces of Canada or from British Columbia, as their rain was equal to or worse than ours. He was impressed with my knowledge and admitted that he was from Alberta, which is on the western edge of the prairie and protected from the Pacific rains by the Coast, Cascade, and Rocky Mountains.

From the meteorological climate, we moved smoothly into the economic climate, which made for interesting comparisons. The world financial situation had affected Canada from the outside—its trading partners capacity to do business had been reduced. As part of Europe, Denmark had taken a bit of a hiding. And then there was Ireland, a member of the infamous PIIGS—Portugal, Ireland, Italy, Greece, and Spain—at the heart of the European fiscal meltdown.

"How did Ireland get to such a level of debt?" Canterbury asked, a reasonable question that was simultaneously naive, simple, and massively complicated. Henrik tensed like an impatient schoolteacher who feels he has explained it all before. I decided to go with "simple."

"It's interesting that the *Titanic* was built in Ireland, as Ireland's story is not unlike that of the ill-fated ship," I began, being intentionally obtuse.

"Well surely you haven't hit the bottom yet," began Charles Canterbury with a look that signaled to all that he was about to say something he judged funny.

"Surely the situation can be *salvaged?*"

I politely laughed. Henrik gave one of his ready-to-laugh looks.

"Actually, my comparison with the *Titanic* is more about the months and hours before it sank than the actual sinking.

"Most people believe that it was the architects, engineers, and designers at the shipyard who had first made the claim that the *Titanic* was unsinkable. It wasn't. The conservative, prudent, and serious-minded Ulstermen behind the project would not have been the sort to make idle claims of invincibility. They had developed a new system of compartmentalization that allowed sections of the ship to be sealed off in the event of a leak. This was a revolutionary safety feature, but it did not guarantee anything.

"This was back in the glory days of the British Empire, when Britannia ruled the waves. A sense of patriotism about any of Britain's achievements ran through all ages and social classes from the miner down a pit to the lord of the manor—and remember, this was at a time when England saw Ireland as a possession. The burgeoning newspaper industry, which was capitalizing on the growth in literacy, was gaining a firm grip on the mood of the country and empire.

"These enormous ocean liners made good copy. They were a combination of high technology and absolute luxury. Just imagine taking *Hello! Magazine* and merging it with the *New Scientist*. Everyone wanted to know about them: brokers, investors, the wealthy travelling elite, engineers and scientists, and the ordinary Joe and Josephine on the street, who could only dream of such a journey.

"Nor was there TV or radio to compete, so magazines and newspapers raced one another to give more astounding facts and intriguing insights into the great ship. So it was a relatively small jump for a hack subeditor, looking for an edge, to turn the sealable compartments into 'unsinkable' ones. This was one of many claims that grew and snowballed, literally leading to an iceberg. I don't think history relates whether or not the engineers at Harland and Wolff shipyard contradicted the claims; they were good for business. After all, these big liners were pretty safe in general. It would take a chance catastrophe to prove the claim wrong.

"At this point, the *Titanic* myth is about where the Irish economy was in 1995. People were talking about the economy as a growing success. And the more people talked, the more citizens, bankers, and politicians believed it.

"Back in 1912 tickets were selling, and the *Titanic* was preparing to launch. But, the tickets weren't sold out. There were tickets to spare, and because of a coal shortage caused by a strike in the mines, passengers from other ships were transferred to the *Titanic* to make better use of available stocks.

"Off they sailed, to be met by enthusiastic crowds in Cherbourg and Cobh before heading out into the North Atlantic.

"By the time she sailed, conversation had probably moved on from the claim that she was unsinkable, but it was a deeply ingrained notion. People believed it beyond a shadow of a doubt.

"So when the first messages about ice tapped through in Morse code, they were treated with less interest than reports about flocks of seagulls would have been. The first message was quite general, along the lines of, 'There are reports of ice fields up ahead.'

"Confident that the *Titanic* was exempt from such warnings, Captain Edward G. Smith stayed to the same course, even though he could have turned to the south. When the second warning came from a nearby ship, the *Baltic,* the captain put it in his pocket, later giving it to J. Bruce Ismay, chairman of the White Star Line. Ismay didn't post the information to the ship's bridge until five hours later.

"The fact that the captain passed the message on shows he must have been a bit anxious. He would have made his employers—White Star—very angry if he'd changed course and slowed the journey or—worse still—let the passengers know why. But as a seasoned sailor, he would have been instinctively respectful of an ice threat. As for Bruce Ismay, what would have been going through his head? Promises made to shareholders? Claims made to government? The profitability and reputation of the entire White Star Line?

"The concerns of these two gentlemen reflect those of the Irish government and the people in charge of banks and other institutions. Sure, there were warnings coming from economists and pundits about an overheating economy, but people were making money. Some were making vast sums. Unemployment, normally a scourge in Ireland, had gone the other way. We had to import labor. Somewhere, a politician or two might have had a warning folded in their pocket, but—excuse the pun—nobody wanted to rock the boat.

"The messages came thick and fast. The sixth, from a ship called the *Mesaba,* warned of a 'vast' belt of ice in a line across their path, a mere seventy-eight miles away. That was less than three hours away for a ship that would have needed several miles to make any meaningful change of direction or reduction in speed.

"Whatever the misgivings of the senior personnel, the more junior officers and sailors were not in the least concerned. That evening, Communications Officer Jack Phillips was tapping out Morse code messages for passengers—greetings, best wishes, and other trivia. He became so incensed by the flood of ice warnings that when the *Californian* wired to say they were stopped and surrounded by ice, he responded with the following message: 'Shut up, shut up. I'm busy, I'm working Cape Race.'

"I distinctly remember, during Ireland's so-called 'Celtic Tiger' years, hearing economist David McWilliams being publicly shouted down by politicians and business people for 'scaremongering' because he warned of the consequences of an overheated economy.

"We all know what happened to the *Titanic*. With Ireland, the iceberg came in the form of the 2008 economic crash, Lehman Brothers being the first of many dominoes to come tumbling down. The Irish people in the lifeboats are those who had money but no debt. In the unsinkable economy, loans had been handed out indiscriminately and well beyond the means of many borrowers. The process has obviously taken longer than the two hours and fifteen minutes it took the *Titanic* to go under, and none of us are really clear as to whether we've hit the bottom yet.

"You could say Ireland now sits suspended in the water, prevented from sinking by the bailouts. What we need is enough buoyancy to get us to the port for repairs."

Henrik gave a hearty chortle. "It is true," he said. "You Irish are good storytellers. And you are also not afraid of, how do you say it, *self-effacement?*"

Charles had a good smile on his face, too.

"Seb, I have to say that story told me more than a six-page article I read in the *Economist*."

We talked some more about this and that, but I eventually realised what time it was. If I were to make good on my promise to get home early, I would have to leave now. It was a bizarre experience to be the one who said he had to leave. When did you last hear of a salesman leaving prospects wanting more? I made sure we exchanged cards and assured both of them I would be calling them—Henrik about the gun club and Charles with details of the hideaway I took my wife to for our anniversary. It's a really good trick, if you can manage to pull it off, to make sure that when you call them the following day or the following week, they have a reason to take your call that isn't something to do with what you're selling.

I went back out to the car. The first thing I did was check my messages. There were a few minor messages about things that I would do on Monday. Another message was from my wife, who wanted me to pick up a few things on the way home. Best of all, there was a call from Dominic to say Alfred wanted to meet next Thursday at 11 a.m. Could I make it? I would delay my own funeral to make it to that meeting.

The window was open, Bruce Springsteen was on the iPod, the sun was setting, and two teenage sons would be relishing the opportunity to put their father to shame over a game of *Modern Warfare*. It had been a great Friday, and Dominic's call was the cherry on the cake.

In a few weeks I would be going on another ride-out, and hopefully Jack would be there. He might not want to talk with me further about my work and his philosophy, but if he did, I had a lot of new material. In addition to the networking meeting and my first meeting with Alfred Kergan, I would have the meeting on Thursday to analyse as well.

A lot of thoughts and ideas were going through my mind. I'd stuck my neck out today. I had walked the plank, asking Laursen about duck hunting and offering to introduce him to the gun club. I'd laid it on quite thick with my *Titanic* story, too, but if you want to make a fire, you blow on sparks where you see them—you don't waste time rubbing wet sticks together.

SHAGGY DOGS AND OLD WIVES

Proper stories are neither fact nor fiction, they are the relating, or re-telling, of events for a purpose – whether that purpose by education, amusement or debate.

It's easy to see why the ancients might have thought the world was flat. The horizon is such a definite thing when it's all you have to look at. If you get to the sea and find the horizon is still ahead of you, how could you possibly envisage anything other than a sheer drop, like Mother Nature's very own infinity pool perched on the edge of an astral cliff?

And, speaking of the creator, on an island as small as Ireland, he had to cram a lot of features into a small space. If you want to have a couple of mountain ranges and a level plain on a journey that is only a hundred and fifty miles coast to coast, those ranges have to be small and that plain has to be narrow.

As I saw the Silvermine Mountains rise up ahead of me on the old Dublin to Cork road, it occurred to me what wishful thinking it had been to call them mountains. This set of mineral-rich bumps nestled between the Cork and Limerick roads was a mere fifteen miles by twenty. My mind went back to the summer I spent working in Canada as a student. I recalled the sheer enormity of the Rockies, which rise as a giant backdrop to the city of Calgary. The city's Sears Tower makes it appear like Oz at the end of the Yellow Brick Road. It took us three days to drive across the Canadian prairie from Ontario to Alberta, and it was mile after mile of unending flatness. Had Christopher Columbus seen it, he would have just eaten the orange and stayed at home.

Oh, how the mind likes to take the scenic route to get to its point. Over the first fifty miles of the ride-out, I had left work behind me. My thoughts had taken the off-ramp from the highway called Work and went wandering through the quaint hills and valleys of family, friends, hopes, ambitions, and motorcycle tuning. Now my thoughts were merging with my workflow again as they took me to Alberta and, inevitably, to Charles Canterbury, Henrik Laursen, and the Chamber of Commerce function.

Henrik had actually phoned me up to ask about the gun club expedition I had mentioned. The way things were headed we would soon find ourselves up to our knees in a swamp, taking swigs of tea from a flask while intermittently firing volleys of lead at airborne Sunday dinners. And at no point in our conversations had I ever mentioned the subject of work or sales.

Spotting the hunter in him seemed to have made an impression. That was no generic professional observation, and introducing him to the gun club wasn't an off-the-shelf corporate entertainment. I had laid the grounds for mutual respect, out of which a business relationship would hopefully grow, and perhaps we could enjoy one another's company, too. And the icing on the cake? He had facilitated a positive connection with Charles Canterbury as well. A productive day's work all around.

The ride-out had met up at a service station just on the edge of the city. Eight men, eight Harley-Davidsons, and a serious serving of sunshine. At this point in the summer, we had all given up two things: one, listening to weather forecasts; two, hope. With our panniers now crammed full of wet gear, we're set to boil in our leathers and layers. I was glad to see Jack, Alan, and Cormac again. Cormac had literally arrived off the ferry that morning

116

with just enough time to fill the laundry basket, have a shower, pack a bag, and eat a sandwich. When he told us this, I made one of my usual comments about remembering his kids' names, and quick as a flash he said:

"Of course I remember my kids' names. Your wife reminds me every time I see her."

Roars of laughter all around and me put in my place. Round one to Cormac! It was a great feeling to be in the sunshine with a group of guys in good moods, all of us anticipating the weekend ahead. Every ride-out is a bonding experience up to a point, but I think our experience in the rain on the last trip had really heightened the sense of camaraderie—the chemistry even spread to the four other guys who hadn't been with us. Max I had met before. He is either a glutton for punishment or he just enjoys a "busman's holiday." He's a mechanic, and I guarantee that between now and 8 p.m. on Sunday night, he'll spend at least two hours on his knees with a spanner, tweaking the tuning on someone else's custom—and not one word of complaint will pass his lips. Gordon "the Shrink" Traynor is a psychiatrist and is always pushed forward as spokesman on the rare occasions we get flagged down by traffic cops. Bertrand is a programmer; I hadn't met him before. Finally there was Brian, a professional dancer and one of the funniest men you are likely to meet. During his early days in the club, everybody had a wisecrack for Brian about being a dancer, but within a very short space of time they gave up teasing him. Nobody could match his razor-sharp wit.

For about twenty minutes we had hung around and talked, drinking coffees and Cokes, either on our feet or sitting on the saddles of our patient motorcycles. Then, without a word being said, we all straddled our mounts and rode out. That had been about an hour and a half earlier, and various physical demands were becoming apparent. I was relieved to see Gordon, who was acting road captain, give the signal for "stop at the next village."

The roads were so beautiful. I've travelled them all my life, to and from Cork or Dublin, but they have always been full of traffic. Over the previous fifteen years, however, motorways had drawn away all of the city-to-city traffic, leaving these wide blacktop roads for local traffic and wayfarers like us to cruise between their hedges, grasses, and loose stone walls. One of the things that had made these roads hell on earth, especially around bank holiday weekends and match days, was the fact that they narrowed as they came to towns and villages, forming the main street. On the other side of town, they widened again. This had caused tailbacks that literally stretched for ten miles at a time. Now, we had the road to ourselves as we hauled into town like a bunch of bandits in a post-modern Western.

Whoever had called for this stop knew the ground. There was a great pub in the village with a garden that went down to the river. Benches and tables were scattered about; it was the perfect place for us to take off our leathers, stretch out in the sun, and have a much-needed meal. One by one, we swung our stiff legs over our bikes and stretched. As we assembled on the grass in our black leathers—some sitting, some standing—it occurred to me that we looked like a consignment of overripe bananas removing our own peels.

I was very hungry and thirsty, so I was pretty much first in line at the serving counter. I then meandered out into the garden with a tray laden with all the things wives know their husbands eat when they're away. A burger made with Angus beef and covered in fried onions and relish, as only a country hotel chef knows how to make it. A plate of fries the size of a prizefighter's fingers. The largest available cup filled with cola. A bowl of something made with overcooked fruit, sugar, and pastry. So focused was I on the food, I scarcely noticed who was sitting where among the scattering of half-peeled, black bananas grilling in the sun. I placed my tray down on one of the tables and began to eat. Apart from the champing of lips, the chiming of cutlery, and the clink of glass, there was little to be heard above the sound of the river as it flowed over the small weir at the end of the pub garden. I was so hungry that I could actually feel my blood sugar increasing as I ate. My mood lifted, and with it, my gaze. I took a closer look at the scene around me.

The tables were made of halved logs and had half-log benches on either side of them—the sort you find in public forests and national parks. Everyone was resolutely eating with their plates still on the trays, so as to avoid the patches of bird droppings decorating the tables. As I looked around, my eyes met Alan's.

"You look engrossed," he said.

"*Gross* is the word," I replied. "I don't know what I was thinking, ordering all of this food."

"So, apart from developing an eating disorder, what's been happening with you since the great flood?"

I had momentarily forgotten that Alan was with us on the last trip, when we camped in the rain and got completely soaked through to the skin. Since I'd been on the bike for a couple of hours, thinking about work, it stood to reason that work was going to be the first thing that came to mind. So, whatever Alan might have expected from his polite enquiry, work is what he got.

"I took over a new position at work a while back. It's put me in front of some pretty big players, and I've been working with a few techniques and theories Jack mentioned during the last ride-out."

"Jack?" he asked.

"Yeah, over there. Big American guy." I indicated him with my fork.

"Oh, that's right. You two were getting quite cosy with one another, if I remember. What sort of techniques? Mind control?"

"Close," I replied. "Storytelling as a multipurpose business tool. The theory is that by taking what you're really trying to say out of the immediate situation and putting it into another context, you invite the listener to focus on the bit that matters. On top of that, the organised, consecutive nature of a story is much easier for people to follow."

"So it's kind of like, 'Once upon a time there was a question. Then along came an answer, and they all lived happily ever after'?"

He wasn't making fun of me. Working with students has made him very upfront and direct. When I first met him, I remember him telling me about the sink-or-swim nature of working with really bright, ambitious students. You have to keep their respect, and, given the fact they're going to correct you on things, you have to keep punching or they'll knock you out of the ring. I thought for a moment.

"I guess storytelling is a bit of a Swiss army knife. Sure, the main blade is there for you to cut to the chase, but you can use it for other things, too."

"Well, yes, I suppose. Like any tools, storytelling will operate differently in different hands. It can be used to explain, to transact, or to exploit," I continued. "But it's also a way to demonstrate aspects of your personality and approach to life—a way to gain trust and win respect."

He laughed.

"You realise you went from stating the potential of stories to 'exploit' to describing them as tools for 'gaining trust and winning respect.' That's an interesting arsenal to carry into professional or social situations."

I was playing with my overcooked fruit, sugar, and pastry confection, with no real commitment to it. Alan pushed his tray away from him, narrowly missing a bird's deposit, and lit up a cigarette. Oh, what a sanctuary the outdoor restaurant or bar is for smokers, who are ostracised from anywhere with a roof. I could tell he was settling in to say a whole heap more, so I didn't bother commenting.

"You know, you've hit on something very ancient and very rich. Stories have always had enormous power, but as a culture or society, we've sort of downgraded them to mere entertainment.

"In my undergraduate year we did a course in anthropology, and I remember the lecturer telling us that storytelling is one of only a handful of human activities that can be traced along the length of time and across the breadth of cultures. In other words, every culture to come before science has or had a tradition of storytelling. It's amazing when you think about it…"

He was flying. Looking around the other tables, I could see we'd all been roused by our feed. Eight guys—large and small—were spread across the lawn, with leather jackets cast aside or jumpsuits peeled back like the aforementioned banana skins. Hopefully no one would make a move for a while; I was enjoying it all.

"I'd never even thought of that," I said. "I'm no anthropologist, but I was kind of aware that every culture tells stories. But look at it another way: if stories are so widespread, and have been for so long…I mean, if they're genuinely universal, they must have an evolutionary role. Even if you're not into evolution, you've got to concede that there must be some sort of survival element necessitating the need to exchange information in that way."

"The evidence goes right back." He waved his cigarette around enthusiastically. "Among the cultures that had written records, there are written stories, whether they be in Sanskrit, Latin, Greek, Chinese, Egyptian, or Sumerian. Then there are the cave drawings. I don't believe those guys went to the trouble of finding indelible dyes and painting those images just because the wife couldn't find wallpaper she liked at the local IKEA. No, those cave images must have been a pretty important story record. But now—now that we can type a badly spelled sentence into our phones and instantly share it with a million people around the globe—storytelling has been reduced to soap operas and soap commercials."

"Hey, Al my pal, you're quite passionate about this, aren't you?"

I laughed to show that I wasn't trying to undermine him.

"Yeah, sorry, Seb. I got a bit carried away, but you're making me think. Perhaps I should be thinking more about storytelling in teaching. I mean, it has applications, not only as a method of imparting and explaining information to students but also as a tool in political engagement."

He stubbed his cigarette out on his boot sole and placed it in the trash, which was a concrete pipe turned up on its end. He was lost in thought. It was very interesting to see how something that had been with each one of us all our lives—storytelling—could look so different to all of us when observed from a different angle. From *Winnie the Pooh* to *War and Peace*, we'd all filed stories on a shelf marked "entertainment." Now, when encouraged to look at the function of stories and their potential application, each of us finds relevance for them in our own field. Powerful stuff.

At that point, Brian the Dancer made his way over to our table and slid onto the bench beside Alan. There is no doubt about it—he is the healthiest one amongst us. Perfect complexion, perfect hair, and, though he was wearing leathers, it was obvious there was a perfect six-pack beneath. No Angus burger with fried onions and relish for him. Oh no, chicken salad—hold the mayo. Once, when I was complaining of being tired and stiff during a ride-out, he told me he'd taken up riding bikes for relaxation, as it was the only time he got to sit down for any length of time.

"So, what are you two looking so intense about, then? Please tell me you're not talking politics again, Alan. You know how wound up you get, and this is supposed to be R & R—rest and recuperation, remember?"

I think I detected a slight blush on Alan's sheepish face. As his cigarette waving intensity a few moments ago showed, he could get quite passionate about things, and given his area of academic specialization, "things" can quite often be politics.

> "No, indeed," Alan responded, with a spring in his verbal stride as he tried to regain his composure. "We were talking about storytelling, believe it or not. Seb here is exploring the use of stories as a sales tool, and I was explaining to him that every culture and civilization known throughout history has had a tradition of storytelling—written or oral."

> "Storytelling relates events in a consecutive and logical order," I chipped in. "This not only helps the listener to understand each new piece of information as it's presented, it also helps them to remember it. It's like creating a verbal dot-to-dot."

Brian showed an interesting combination of hesitation and impatience— impatience with himself—as he gathered his thoughts. It was as if the subject had never occurred to him before, but now that it was in front of him, it seemed very familiar.

> "Bear with me on this one, OK?" he began, releasing his impatience. "But dance is a form of storytelling too, and it's not just humans that do it. I mean, once you look at how animals behave, you see that the only difference between the way our species tells stories and the way they're told by the rest of the animal kingdom is that we use pictures and sounds."

Alan was trying to keep a straight face. I could see he'd found a way of getting back at Brian for the politics comment. He couldn't hold back.

> "So let me get this straight, Brian. Tchaikovsky just translated his version of *Swan Lake* from the original swan?"

Brian didn't miss a beat.

"I can't speak for *Swan Lake*, but what about Rimsky-Korsakov's *Flight of the Bumblebee*. How do you think bees tell each other where to find nectar? They dance."

He paused to let it sink in.

"It's called a 'Waggle Dance,' and—as the name suggests—they waggle. The combination of their movements and the angle of the sun communicates where there is a source of nectar, water, pollen, or a new home. Is that a story? Yes, it is. A simple one, but it's a story expressed through interpretive dance."

"Rubbish. A bee waggling its ass is not a story," Alan retorted.

"Where's the status quo that's challenged and changed? How is the world a different place afterwards?"

"Status quo: no nectar. Challenge: the bees must search for a new source. They go and find the nectar. They survive," Brian said, defending his theory.

"But it's not a story. It's a series of events in a story, maybe, but they aren't not a story."

Alan was not going to be convinced.

I wasn't going to get involved. I did find the idea of bees doing interpretive dance funny. I was getting images of peacocks and birds of paradise, remembering my thoughts at the Chamber of Commerce charity event. Brian went on.

"The critical thing for me—I mean, the reason it's a story—is that the bees have to interpret the literal direction and distance from symbols of the dance. In humans, the ability to achieve this level of thought doesn't occur until after the age of three. It requires what's called 'Theory of Mind.' That is not to suggest that bees have the same level of deductive and reasoning powers as humans, just that they are able to relate information to one another."

A few moments ago, we had been marvelling at the fact that all human civilisations utilised stories, and now insects were using them. What would be next? I didn't have to wait long before Alan made his contribution to what had been a discussion but was about to look more like an argument.

"That is such a load of hippy nonsense," Alan said, shaking his head.

"Next you'll be telling me that the cooing sounds from the pigeon in my back garden are actually computer code or that my dog is actually signalling in semaphore when she wags her tail. I mean, where does it end? When a dog lifts his leg on a lamppost, perhaps that's telling a story too. I can just see it now, *The Lamp Post* by A. Barker: 'Once upon a time, I was here. I'm a male Rottweiler about the size of a pony, and this is my turf. If you're a male dog and you're smaller than a pony, you might want to turn around. If you're a female dog—how you doin'? Here's my pheromone number. Maybe we can live happily ever after.'"

Alan was flying now. He would have gone on if Brian hadn't come back in right away.

"Exactly. I couldn't have put it better myself. That's exactly the point I'm making. Animals and plants communicate messages to one another in a logical, consecutive manner through a variety of mediums—one being dance, others being images, song, colour, and words. As far as we know, words are the only thing that distinguishes our communication from the rest of the world's species."

It was always good fun to watch Alan and Brian joust with one another. They were so different in so many ways, but both of them depended on agility and speed for their professional survival. Though Brian's agility was primarily his footwork and Alan's his intellect, the quickness of their respective wits was evidence of the fact that alertness begins in the mind, regardless of which component of our bodies expresses it. Without conceding that Brian's point might be a valid one, Alan sidestepped with a story of his own.

"The ancient Greeks were great people for stories," he began. "And, come to think of it, they often used them the way you're talking about, Seb—allegorically and instructively. When Plato felt that the Athenians were getting vain, lazy, and too full of themselves, thus making themselves vulnerable to attack or decay, he didn't stand on a soapbox wagging his finger. He didn't shout out, 'Repent, all ye sinners!' Instead, he told the story of Atlantis—a hugely successful city that was probably the city of Akrotiri on the island of Thera, which was destroyed by the largest volcanic eruption in human history. Plato borrowed and embellished the legend of the city's destruction to deliver a warning about what happens when you get too big for your boots. But my favourite story from ancient Greece concerns Socrates—or as Bill and Ted referred to him, 'So-Crates.'

"Socrates lived between 469 BC and 399 BC and was widely renowned as a bit of a clever clogs. People would come to him and seek his advice on matters of philosophy, religion, justice, and love. And when there weren't people actively seeking his advice, he'd go to the *agora*, or marketplace, stand on an orange crate, and dish out advice to anyone who would listen.

"One morning, as Socrates was sitting on his stoop—whittling, stitching a hole in a toga, or doing whatever philosophers did in their downtime—Dexicos, an acquaintance of his, ran up to him breathlessly and said, 'Socrates, you know what I just heard about Diogenes?'

"To which Socrates replied, 'Hold on there one darn second, Dexicos. Before you tell me, I'd like you to pass a little test. It's called the Triple Filter Test.'

126

"'Triple filter?' asked Dexicos.

"'That's right, my friend,' Socrates went on. 'Before telling me about Diogenes, let me help you filter what you have to say. First of all, the Truth filter—are you positive that what you want to tell me is true?'

"'Er, not exactly, no,'" Dexicos answered in rather coy voice. 'Actually, I just heard about it.'

"'*Ola kala,*' said Socrates, or OK, as we say nowadays. 'So you don't really know if it's true? Then let's try the second filter—the filter of Goodness. Is what you want to tell me about Diogenes something good?'

"Dexicos was more confident in his answer this time. 'No, on the contrary, Socrates...'

"'So,' Socrates continued. 'You want to tell me something about Diogenes that may be bad, even though you're not certain it's true?'

"Dexicos shrugged. He was a little embarrassed, but above all, he thought that Socrates was being a bit of a killjoy. Socrates went on.

"'You may still pass the test, though, because there is a third filter, the filter of Usefulness. Is what you want to tell me about Diogenes going to be useful to me?'

"'No, not really.' Dexicos had lost all interest in the conversation and was now thinking about the game of backgammon and bottle of retsina he was having with another, less pedantic, friend that afternoon.

"'Well,' concluded Socrates rather pompously, 'If what you want to tell me is neither true nor good nor even useful, why tell it to me, or anyone at all?'

"Dexicos pretended to look humbled, bewildered, and ashamed, but under his breath he muttered, 'Suit yourself, Socrates.' After all, Socrates might have been a great philosopher who was held in high esteem across the known world, but he had just passed up the opportunity to find out that Diogenes was having an affair with his wife."

As if our laughter had broken their reverie, a movement began among the group, and one by one the guys stood up, stretched, and zipped on their leathers. Helmets on, visors snapped into place, and one by one, the unmistakeable sound of Harley engines firing up began. *Thrummm.* I left Brian and Alan and wandered towards my bike. I wanted my mind to be focused on the more serious matters while I was on the road, but it was going to be interesting to see if the conversation continued when we stopped for the night. That's the one of the funny things about a ride-out. You have a conversation with someone, then you put on your helmet and sit on a bike for two hours, where you inevitably pick over the conversation and come up with a whole heap of other points. By the time you get to talk again, you're both ready to take the topic back into the ring for another round.

I smiled as I approached my bike, noticing again the perfect angle at which the bikes were parked, with each front mudguard a genteel fifteen degrees to the kerb. I took one more helping of light and a big lungful of air before pulling the helmet down over my face. It's actually very comfortable and well ventilated, but I have an ever-so-slight tendency towards claustrophobia, which I have to conquer every time I encase my head. It's an irrational fear small enough to be overcome by rational thought. One by one we peeled off from the kerb and picked up where we'd left off on the main street. Every time we're in that situation—a pod or swarm of motorcycles cruising through a built-up area, our oversized engines growling with menace—I'm thrown back to all those movies I used to watch as a teenager: *Mad Max, Rollerball,* and *Terminator.* In my mind's eye, a panicking citizen has just preceded us, running down the street while ringing a handbell and shouting, "Lock up your daughters!" I wondered how the good folk of this small town—estimated population five thousand—perceived us? They didn't seem that bothered, nor had they reason to be. Far from *The Good, the Bad, and the Ugly*, their town was under threat from nothing more fearsome than a dancer, a salesman, a psychiatrist, a truck driver...you get the picture.

We were heading for Ballybunion, a seaside holiday resort on the southwest coast, famous for its surfing beach and two golf courses, one of which was more famous than the other because Bill Clinton played there a few weeks before admitting he'd "had relations with that woman." None of us are golfers or surfers—one obsessive hobby at a time, please—but we had discovered, through conversation, that none of us had been there, and all of us were curious about it. Not that we were giving ourselves much of a chance to explore the place. We would probably arrive around 6:30 p.m. and we were scheduled to leave at 11 a.m. the next day, but I repeat, we are bikers as opposed to golfers or surfers.

Our route would take us through some spectacularly beautiful villages and landscapes, along the estuary, and out to the open Atlantic shore. As I think I've said before—and I have no shame in repeating it—Ireland certainly manages to cram in a great variety of landscapes and features into a very small space. I drank in the view as we passed: lush fields grazed by fat, healthy cows nonchalantly staring at us. Our engines grumbled in frustration at the reduced speed, which was necessitated by the tight corners of the road as it twisted between the dry stone walls. I began thinking about Alan and Brian, jousting with each other—each determined to assert his own fixed opinion while opposing that of the other. The truth was that they had both confirmed the universality of stories. Whether or not you interpreted a bee's dance as a story was irrelevant.

Frankly, my only real interest in the subject was how I could use storytelling as a device to further my case in sales. I had missed so many opportunities and lost so many sales for the wrong reasons. I'd done a lot of courses over the years, I'd been taught a lot of methods and techniques, and I'd been given a lot of anecdotal evidence, but this was the first time I actually had a full, 360-degree concept that—as far as I could see—would enable me to address all of my problem areas. I wasn't interested in hypnotizing people and talking them into buying things they didn't need. I'm not the

129

guy who wants to sell fridges in Greenland or sand in Arabia. I'm just the guy who wants to tell the truth better, and—even more importantly—to be understood when I tell it.

Obviously I wasn't in a position to interview any bees about their story-telling methodology, but the notion of how universal stories are among cultures and civilizations was running around the inside of my helmet. It occurred to me that martial-arts movies were always riddled with stories—cryptic stories populated by cranes, praying mantis, snakes, and of course the infamous grasshopper. From what I can tell, Native American lore is also full of stories explaining how things happen. I remember as a child, my grandparents would tell me stories to explain things. Even as a six–year-old, I don't think I was convinced they were true; all the same, the stories had a trajectory, a journey. The story would begin from the premise set by a question I had asked. My grandparents would then set up a scenario in which something happened that answered my question. The story would conclude with the usual:

"And that's why…blah-blah."

In the next county over from where I grew up, there's a mountain called the Devil's Bit, a name guaranteed to have a story behind it, and one certain to rouse the curiosity of a child. When I asked my grandfather about it once, he began with:

"Well you see now…," which has to be one of the oddest sentences committed to print and a sentence only an Irish person would utter.

"Well you see now, that's on account of the Devil and God having an argument about who was the strongest."

He pointed towards the skyline, where a long escarpment ran from left to right of our field of vision, uninterrupted but for one gap gouged out of the rock. From a distance it looked small, but up close it was appreciable.

" 'I made the mountains,' said God.

"'That's nothing,' said the Devil, 'I can knock them down.' And with that, the Devil went over to that line of hill over there and began trying to prise a piece of rock out of it. He tugged away with both of his gnarly hands for seven days and seven nights before anything budged. Then, at last, he came away with a piece of rock, leaving that gap there."

In a way that only grandparents can, he spoke with casual authority and a face as straight as a ruler.

"Well, of course God wasn't impressed at all. Not even a little bit. To the Devil he said, 'It took you seven days and seven nights to lift that one pebble out of the mountainside. Sure didn't I build the whole world in six and spend the seventh day resting?'

"The Devil wasn't one bit happy about being beaten. He lifted the piece of rock and drew it back behind his shoulder and said to God, 'Since you're so great and mighty, catch this, why don't you?' And with that, the Devil gave an almighty throw that sent the rock through the air. God didn't so much as flinch as his eyes followed the rock to where it landed between his feet.

"'Thank you,' said God to the Devil. 'That would be a fine place for a monastery!'

"'So that hole in the hillside above is where the Devil lifted the stone, and the Rock of Cashel is where it landed.'"

With a twinkle in his eye, my grandfather concluded his bogus geography-cum-geology lesson.

The Rock of Cashel is rock rising out of the plain, on which sits a medieval monastery, and this was my grandfather's enchanting way of explaining how it came to be. As rational twenty-first century human beings, it's a quaint story. But remember, we have benefited from sufficient education that enables us to read and write. We also have access to instantaneous information from the world via radio, TV, telephone, and Internet. Back when that story was first cooked up, however, the audience for which it was intended would have taken it as fact. While it might have been conceived in fun, the story would have been designed to achieve a few goals—mostly religious ones.

On a primary level it localized God, reinforcing the idea that while the stories of the Judeo-Christian Bible took place in The Middle East, the people of medieval Ireland were living in the same world and were created by the same God. It suggested that God and the Devil were physical presences—and giants, to boot. Importantly, it stressed that God was more powerful than the Devil and that God was not intimidated by the Devil. Ironically, from the storyteller's point of view, the least important aspect of the story was the fact that it answered the question(s), *Why is there a gap in that hill?* or *Why is the Rock of Cashel there?*

Funny. When my Grandfather told me that story, he was telling a fairy story, a bit of blarney. Thirty years later I'm analyzing it, and I now realize it was a piece of religious propaganda used either by priests or chieftains to keep people frightened, loyal, and faithful.

With these thoughts going through my mind, I suddenly began to sense the sea. A mixture of salt, iodine, and ozone was making its way through the vents of my helmet. A sea breeze has to be the most invigorating way to inhale oxygen. It tastes of life, it feels like energy, and it makes the heart rise in your chest. Was it a reminder that life began in the oceans? A call back to our primordial roots? Or was it simply the fact that this air had had nothing to pollute it, bar a few ships' funnels, over the four thousand miles of ocean ahead of me.

We had been stretched out along the road for the last while, and I had spent much of the journey without any other riders in view. As our route merged with the coast road into the town, we began to slow down and cluster, partly to be ready for any hand signals or impending powwow but largely because we all wanted to absorb the view and the air. It was six o'clock on a June evening. The sun was still up in the sky, but it was signaling its intent to descend towards the horizon as it made its way out over the ocean for its breakfast appointment in New York. The self-conscious grumble of the slowing Harley engines was heard again as we slowed down through the village, sloping in single file down the ramp-like road to the beach. A group of small children with crab-laden buckets stood, backs to the wall, watching in awe as we passed. There was a small, ragged, concrete parking platform just above beach level, its walls painted yellow to remind late-night lovers or fisherman to stop their cars before they found themselves wedged irretrievably in the sand of the beach. There was one car parked there, denying us the symmetry of eight bikes in a row along the yellow wall at fifteen degrees. Instead, we had to park in an unaccustomed chaos.

The beach was absolutely beautiful—a classic seaside beach from a children's storybook. A river weaved its way across the sand, creating an artist's impression of a delta before being absorbed into the anonymity of the sea a hundred and fifty yards away. On either side, headlands stood like great shoulders of rock as gateposts to the bay, one crowned with a now-ruined castle tower. There was no one on the beach, and the virgin sand stretched out to the foam, daring us to press our boot prints into its golden perfection.

Part of me wanted to head to the hotel—to get changed into shorts and trainers so I could take them off and feel the sand against my bare feet. I resisted the temptation. We were being spontaneous, and I knew we would all be heading back soon enough for showers before dinner. A shortsighted onlooker watching from above the beach might have mistaken us for divers as we swaggered down the ramp in our mostly black leathers, leaving sixteen trails of boot prints across the pure sand.

It took me a couple of minutes to acclimatize. After hours in my helmet-cocoon, I had to readjust to being among people. Others don't take so long. Just ahead of me, Brian and Alan were hard at it already, with Gordon the Shrink walking in stride with them, listening with an air of curiosity and amusement. I sped up so that I could join them.

"Are you guys still arguing about bees, dogs, and lamp posts?" I said, almost hoping they were on another topic.

Gordon answered.

> "They're arguing about whether bees can tell stories or something. I have heard of a 'spelling' bee but not a 'telling' bee. I'm not an animal behaviorist but I will say this much: there's a strong physiological element to stories and how the brain receives and responds to them."

The great thing about someone like Gordon is that he's very hard to contradict. I'm not saying he lords it over you or anything, but when we get to discussing subjects he knows about there aren't any grey areas. He just knows stuff that none of the rest of us do. Alan may be an academic, but I can argue with him about politics because it involves opinions as much as facts.

> "Well, go on Gordon, don't leave us hanging," Alan said.

> "Well, I guess that's a response in itself," I said. "Gordon has stimulated an appetite for information to be supplied, expanded, and concluded!"

Gordon picked up a large stick of kelp from the sand. You know you're beside a real ocean when you find seaweed like that—strong trunk-like stems sturdy enough to hold their own against the Atlantic swell.

> "First of all," Gordon began, "there are the four core responses to stories—and, let's be honest, to information in general."

Using the kelp stalk, he drew a circle and put the word "story" in the middle of it. Above it he wrote "rational," below it "physiological," and on either side he wrote "neurological" and "emotional."

> "When it comes to receiving stories, these are the four points of the brain's compass. And for what it's worth, you guys, these elements are present in animals as well as humans. Our rational mind processes the story in its context. For example, when we hear the

story of the *Tortoise and the Hare*, we automatically allow for the fact that tortoises and hares don't talk to one another or place bets—as far as we know. Interestingly, while our rational mind might allow animals to speak, it will not tolerate inconsistency. If the tortoise is wearing pink lipstick at the starting line and not at the finishing line, the story will be rejected or at least compromised."

He then drew an arc around to the word 'emotional.'

"Whether we like it or not, we have emotional responses: sympathy, empathy, like, dislike. These responses can be borne out of rational or physiological deductions, but they are still emotions. You may feel sorry for the tortoise because you know he's at a disadvantage or dislike the hare because he's arrogant. All of these factors will influence your ultimate response and reaction to the story being told."

Gordon walked around to the 'neurological' side. He was enjoying having an audience. Jack had joined us; Bertrand, Max, and Cormac were down at the water's edge looking for stones to skim or collecting seashells or something.

"Now there's the neurological, the more physical flip side to emotion. While your emotions remain largely in your head, your neurons send out messages to the four corners of your body—prompting shivers down the spine, tears, clenched knuckles, and so forth, all of which are physiological responses to the story."

He walked dramatically to the south pole of his drawing, the "physiological."

"So, if a chieftain wants to make his warriors fight more fiercely— a physiological action—he tells them a story about how the enemy has destroyed their crops, leveled their homes, and stolen their women, leaving their children hungry and homeless."

Discussion broke out immediately. Brian was first in, with a simple question: "But as you said yourself, these responses apply to any information received by the brain. How do we know it relates specifically to stories?"

I was surprised at the doubt in Brian's voice. After all, Gordon's illustration backed up his point of view. As expected, Gordon had a ready answer.

"As we psychiatrists are so fond of saying, 'There's been a lot of work done in this area.' We can now measure brain activity and present it through images. Studies have identified the areas that are stimulated during storytelling. Got a pen and paper? Here are some of them: the medial and lateral prefrontal cortex, the cingulate cortex, the temporoparietal junction, and the temporal poles. These guys all light up sequentially as stories are told. And we now know where the stimulus takes place, whether it's the left or right—logical or creative—side of the brain."

"Yes, but what is that telling us?" Alan asked.

"It tells us that the brain likes stories because they package information for processing across the departments of the brain: rational, intuitive, somatic, and emotional. It's a sort of informational bento box."

"So as regards animals," Brian said pensively, "this process either *does* happen for them, or, if it doesn't, it's one of the traits that gives us an advantage over other life forms?"

Gordon nodded as Jack, who had been uncharacteristically quiet all this time, said:

"I guess if we can have old wives' tales, they can have their shaggy dog stories."

There was a good-natured groan from the five of us. Then Gordon said:

"Speaking of animals, there's a story that helps explain how delivering information in a fable or story format helps to make that information useful by putting it into a context the listener can understand and relate to."

He coughed lightly and then began.

"One sun-dappled autumn afternoon, a man was driving along a beautiful, winding country lane. The hedgerows on either side of the lane were lush and high, and the light of the lowering sun danced through the gaps in the leaves, making it hard to see around any of the corners.

"He had his window down to gain full advantage of the aromatic summer air. Like his car, his mind meandered, mainly around thoughts of the rather beautiful girl he was supposed to meet in five minutes' time. He was still a twenty-minute fast drive away. Little did he know that a car was approaching from the opposite direction, also in a hurry, and also with its window down. The only difference was that it was driven by a young woman.

"At speed, the two cars and their drivers approached the final bend and were only just able to slow down in time to avoid a collision. As the screeching of brakes rang in their ears, they tentatively eased their vehicles past one another, narrowly avoiding any scrapes to the paintwork of their respective cars.

"As the two open windows aligned, the woman turned and shouted to the man, 'Pig!' To which, quick as a flash, he replied, 'Cow!'

"In a blaze of indignation and chauvinistic mutterings, he accelerated around the corner...and crashed headlong into a pig."

Amid a mixture of more groans and genuine laughter, Gordon delivered the summary of his story:

"The word 'pig' is not a story. It has no use without a context."

It was time to head for our hotel, whose name reflected the area's golfing reputation: the Nine Iron Inn. Cormac, Max, and Bertrand had joined us now, and we made our way back to the bikes.

The Nine Iron Inn was about a mile and a half outside the town. We had already decided to contain our night's revelry within the hotel bar rather than venture into the town. We were all pretty tired and had agreed that an early night and an early breakfast in the town would give us a chance to explore the area a bit before heading out on the road again.

It was a small hotel with big, luxurious rooms. The room I was sharing with Brian had a great view of the golf course and the sea. After a good pebble dashing from the power-shower, I headed downstairs for a much-anticipated beer. Jack, Cormac, and Alan were already there, beers in hand.

"Well, Seb, you seem to have the whole ride-out debating the merits of stories," Cormac began.

"I had never thought about it before, but now that we're talking about it, it seems obvious that stories can be used to convince people of stuff. I mean, look at religion. The guys with the best stories get more followers."

I knew that the parables Jesus tells in the Christian New Testament were an important part of communicating the gospel, but I hadn't extrapolated to other religions and faiths. Before I could say anything, Jack chipped in.

"I'd say the 'most effective' stories, not the 'best' stories. I mean, the Good Samaritan parable gets its message across, but when I've got time on my hands, I'd rather pick up a John Grisham or a Dan Brown novel."

"Now that you mention it, what was that story trying to say, anyway?" Cormac said quizzically.

I'll admit, I'd never really thought about it. I'd just had it pushed at me as a kid in Catholic school. Bertrand, who had just joined, gave his answer.

"It was trying to say that we shouldn't judge people on appearances. The other people in Israel didn't trust Samaritans, and the story shows that everyone should get a chance."

"Hadn't he just said 'Love thy neighbor' or something and someone asked, 'Who is my neighbor?' and the story was an explanation?"

You could tell by the awkward way Cormac phrased it that he knew his stuff but didn't want to be seen as a Bible expert. He went on more confidently.

"If he'd come out and said, 'Everyone is your neighbor, even the Samaritans,' he would have got laughed at or even stoned..." At this, there was a ripple of laughter.

"You know what I mean. He would have had stones thrown at him. So he told the story of someone perceived of as bad doing something good and left it to the listeners to decide."

This was absolutely on the money. This was a perfect illustration of how a story packages information and enables you to point the listener in the direction you want them looking while leaving them to make their own decisions. And, while Jesus might have been doing this to avoid ridicule or injury, it also works in the sales context. If you tell a prospect a story that channels their needs, your product benefits, and their market factors all in the right direction, you can leave them to make up their own minds, rather than badgering and cajoling them. I jumped in.

"We are always more ready to believe something we have concluded for ourselves rather than an opinion put upon us. It's something you learn in sales."

"So you're saying Jesus was a salesman?" Brian said tauntingly.

"Darn right he was," said Jack. "Collectively, Christians, Jews, Muslims, Sikhs, and Buddhists account for well over half the world's population. And those religions are all based on stories. That's four and a half billion people who have bought into stories. And if they are prepared to stake their eternal souls on a bunch of stories, storytelling is a pretty powerful thing, don't you think?

With Jack, you don't know whether he's being funny, provocative, or just telling it like he sees it. He had either made them all think or he'd offended them, because there was a brief pause before another word was said.

That word was, "Dinner?"

BREAKFAST OF CHAMPIONS

Harleys don't have hoods but stories do. Get under the hood of a well crafted story and you'll see how it sparks.

If you have never heard the sound of a peacock, my wish for you is that you never do. Every ounce and shade of beauty they present—their iridescent blueness, the hundred gleaming eyes that stare in surprise from their fan of feathers, their noble crests—is out weighed a hundredfold by the sheer, persistent ugliness of their voices.

I know that *now*. But at seven o'clock that Sunday morning, all I knew about peacocks was that they had loads of feathers but are useless at flying. As planned, we had all retired early; that is, if you call half past eleven early. I had fallen like a felled cedar and slept like the proverbial log right the way through, only to be exploded into consciousness by what sounded like a thousand angry seagulls with bronchitis. Indeed, I think I was actually in mid-air before I woke up, such was my shock. As I ran to the window, I collided with Brian, who was on a similar mission. Arriving at the window, I expected to find one of those strange, winged devils that crop up in horror movies or, at the very least, a cat being masticated by a Rottweiler. Instead, we found ourselves being eyeballed by a slightly tilted, crowned blue head surrounded by the most beautiful semicircle of green iridescence I have ever seen. As we took in the scene, I realized that I was nearly hyperventilating. I looked along to the next window, from which Brian was inspecting the bird. I could see his chest heaving rhythmically, too.

"Well, I guess a lie in is out of the question. I don't think I'll be calm enough to sleep before November," Brian gasped.

"True that!" I wheezed.

I decided to go for a walk and give Brian a turn in the shower. I'd see the lay of the land, if the others had—miraculously—managed to stay asleep, it could be a while before they came downstairs. Sometimes I like to take breakfast alone, but today I was in a sociable mood. Eating together is a good way to iron out any glitches or changes in plan before hitting the road.

"I'm going out to strangle that bird," I joked. "The shower's yours."

"For God's sake, don't do that," he replied. "If they make that sound under normal circumstances, I most certainly don't want to hear what they sound like when they're being strangled!"

There was nobody downstairs in the lobby or at reception, though there was a distant kitchen-like clatter signaling the source of the baking smells filling the air. The aroma of freshly baked bread is exquisite, but as I went out the front door, I was met by something sweeter—the fresh morning breeze off the ocean. The extraordinary, tingling exhilaration I felt breathing that air immediately dispelled the tension that had gripped my whole body since hearing the peacock.

There is something very evocative about the seaside in the morning. The low angle of the sun causes its rays to hit the sides of ripples and waves, creating shimmering reflections like a field of diamonds swaying in the breeze. I followed the gravel path around to the back of the building. I had no evil intent to execute the peacock; I just wanted to see it closer up, though I hoped it would keep its beak closed. There was a paddock with a couple of very handsome horses in it, and as I approached it, I noticed a man leaning against the white-iron rail, tobacco pipe in hand, observing the animals. This, it appeared, was the grassy spot beneath our window, and sure enough, there was the peacock. I addressed the man.

"I thought I'd come and get a closer look at the banshee," I said.

He knew what I meant immediately. Without turning his head, he replied.

"Wake you, did he? If they're a minute late with the saucer of meal for him, he begins that caterwauling!"

"Caterwauling!" I grunted. "I have never heard that word better applied. That was a caterwaul if ever I heard one."

"Tell me," he asked, "do you know why they can't fly, the peacocks?"

He had a wonderful, chocolaty texture to his voice. It was like listening to Richard Burton or James Earl Jones, only with a pronounced rural Irish accent. He paused, giving me time for my inevitable answer of *no*.

"Well, years ago, there was a blackbird and a peacock in the village, and each of them had a broken wing. They knew that in time their wings would fix themselves, but it was hard work hopping around after food and harder work still trying to escape the jaws of the fox and the cat."

He took a pull on his pipe, his voice becoming smoother and deeper as he spoke through an exhalation of smoke.

"One evening, while watching from his tree, the blackbird noticed some goings on at the fairy ring. In daytime it was just a circle of mushrooms in the pasture, but of a full moon, it would be filled with fairies dancing and leaping.

"The fairies only had drums to accompany their dance, so the blackbird chipped in with a few harmonious notes of his own. And when the dancing was done and all the other birds were preparing for the dawn chorus, the fairies thanked the blackbird and asked him if he had any wishes. 'I do indeed,' said the blackbird. 'I wish my wing were full again.' And before two bars of dawn chorus had sounded, the blackbird was flying up this way and down that.

"A few days later, the peacock asked him how he had managed to heal his wing so quickly, and the blackbird told him. At the next full moon, the blackbird looked down from his tree, only to see the peacock waiting impatiently at the fairy ring.

"When the dancing started, the peacock began his roaring and screeching. After less than a minute, the fairies stopped their dancing. 'In the name of all that's holy,' said the king of the fairies. 'What are you making that noise for?'

"His neck straight and his beak in the air, the peacock arrogantly explained he was helping with the dance, and in return, he wanted the fairies to mend his broken wing.

"At that, the king of the fairies laughed. 'The blackbird made our dance better, so we made his wing better,' he said. 'You have made our song worse, and you know what that means? You can have the break we took from his wee wing.'

"And ever since then, the peacock has had two almost useless wings."

I laughed. I hadn't heard a story told like that since my grandfather had told me ones like the Devil's Bit story. He had the same air of authority, and he told the story in the same deadpan way, just as he would have described a football game or a motor accident. And I told him as much. The story lifted me so much I had almost forgiven the peacock. Almost.

144

I stayed there about ten minutes chatting with the man before strolling around and watching a few dawn golfers making their way around the links. In other circumstances I would have been itching to get out there for a full eighteen holes. With a full day ahead of me I could probably beat Bill Clinton's round. But this morning I just wanted to drink in more of the air and then get back on my bike.

The gravel made a satisfying crunch under my feet as I wandered back around to the front entrance. Baking smells emerged from the front door just ahead of the voices. Everyone was there except Brian and Max, who were still showering. I had evidently arrived just as a debate was concluding. Gordon appointed himself spokesperson.

"The feeling is, it would be nice to go and have breakfast somewhere in the town, as we didn't really get to see the place last night."

"That sounds like a plan," I said, adding, "It had better be soon or I'll end up eating someone's saddlebag!"

We had a consensus and we were satisfied that the other guys would be happy enough. We all went back to our rooms, packed, and returned to settle our bills.

"You'll not stay for breakfast, gentlemen?" asked the woman swiping our credit cards. I guessed she was the woman of the house. The traces of flour around her cuticles and the look of disappointment on her face told me she had assumed we would be staying and was baking for our benefit.

"Not this time. We have to hit the road," we chorused guiltily before shuffling out the door to our mounts.

Assumptions are dangerous things, especially on an empty stomach. We'd assumed that since it was June and we were in a holiday town with golf and surfing, we would have a choice of places to have breakfast at 7:30 a.m. Evidently this was not the case. We trundled down the main street at a pace that kept our engine noise low and gave us a chance to scope what was on offer. We all saw a hotel and simultaneously drew in to the kerb, assuming we had found what we were looking for. We barely had the Harleys on their stands before we heard the loud screech of a large but ill-fitting sash window being pulled up above our heads.

A bald head, shrouded by thick, black sideburns and a moustache, emerged, followed by a rug-like bare chest—*bear* chest, even. Thankfully, only the waistband of a pair of brown, boogie-nights briefs was visible over the top of the windowsill. A voice, with a much thicker accent than my storytelling friend, bellowed something incomprehensible at us. Being closest to the window, I cupped my ear and replied, as courteously as I could:

"I'm sorry?"

The reply was equally incomprehensible, though this time I could tell he was shouting to be heard rather than out of real anger.

"I'm sorry, did we wake you?" I shouted back.

This time, his voice and accent were as clear as a newsreader from NBC, CNN, or BBC.

"*Yes!*"

"Probably time you were getting up anyway!" I yelled, hoping his good humor could identify my good humor at this distance. I weighed up the time it would take him to run down the stairs in his porn-star undies against the zero-to-sixty in four seconds that our bikes could do. Seeing he hadn't decided to come down and challenge me, I asked, "Anywhere around here you'd recommend for breakfast?"

"There's another hotel at the end of the street on your left. They'll probably be serving in twenty minutes or so. They'll do you a proper fry-up."

146

Either I had become acclimatized to his accent or this was his wide-awake voice, as I could now understand everything. I had no idea whether he was a guest, an employee, or the proprietor of the hotel. Whichever it was, he had just directed eight out-of-towners with significant disposable incomes to a competing establishment. Even so, I made a mental note of the place. He was a very entertaining guy, if I could only erase the image of the hairy chest and boogie-nights briefs.

"Much appreciated!" I shouted. "Sorry we woke you up!"

I had two reasons for shouting this: one, so that the man in the window could hear; two, so that the rest of the village could hear, as we had probably woken them as well.

Before we turned around to get back on our bikes, he shouted again.

"That's no problem. Beautiful bikes, by the way. Really nice!"

"Thanks!" we said together, conscious that he was still there, elbows on the windowsill, waiting to watch us head off up the street in search of that fry-up.

As it turned out, the other hotel was so close to our previous stop we could probably have continued our conversation with the guy in the window. We self-consciously dismounted, aware that two stops and starts in five minutes had likely ensured the attention of everyone from surfers on their way to the beach to local pensioners catching up on gossip. We were probably now a main topic of conversation.

Inside the hotel it was very dark after the morning light outside. We were ushered into a dining area. Based on the lingering smell of stale beer and sweat, it must have hosted some form of dance or function the previous night. The smell made me nostalgic for the Nine Iron Inn and the fresh baking we'd left behind. We quickly placed our order—"Eight full Irish with coffee"—and soon the morning-after odor was chased out into the sunlight by the mouthwatering tang of frying bacon. I was sitting between

Jack and Gordon. I was glad to be near Jack, as we had hardly spoken on this trip, and I was looking forward to catching up.

"So, Seb," Cormac said from the other side of the table.

"Is this story thing going to win you a Noble Prize for literature or what?"

"I'm working on it, I'm working on it," I replied, smiling as I thought of our exchange the previous day.

"Did you ever hear the story about the mechanic and the heart surgeon?" Cormac asked.

We shook our heads, remaining silent in anticipation. Cormac is a good raconteur.

"A mechanic was in his shop one day, on his knees in front of a motorcycle. He was gently removing a cylinder head from its motor when he heard a customer come through the door. He reverentially laid the cylinder head on the bench and approached the reception desk. As he got closer, he recognized the customer as a well-known heart surgeon. You know, the sort of semi-celebrity type that the radio stations and newspapers go to for quotes, who pretend to be modest and shy but are actually lapping it up. On that basis, the mechanic thought he'd make a gentle dig. Nothing rude or unkind that might lose the doctor as a customer, just a little bit of banter. The doctor had picked out a pair of gauntlets from a display rack, and it was simply a matter of swiping his credit card. As he did so, the mechanic said, 'Hey, Doc, can I ask you a question?'

"'Absolutely,' the doctor replied in his media-savvy tone.

"'So, Doc, you see that engine over there? I open its heart, take valves out, fix 'em, put 'em back in, and when I'm finished, the engine works just like new.'

"He paused for effect, handing the gauntlets in a bag and the credit card back to the doctor.

"'So how come I get paid buttons and you get the really big bucks. We're basically doing the same thing?'

"The surgeon paused, smiled, leaned over the counter, and whispered to the mechanic...'Try doing it with the engine running!'"

Our sudden laughter caused those at the other end of the table to pause and look up to see what was happening. Cormac began talking with Gordon on his other side, and Jack leant towards me and said, "So, is it making any difference?"

My mind was still with the mechanic and the surgeon, so I had to ask him what he meant.

"The storytelling. Is it making any difference to your business?" he said, as if it were the most obvious thing in the world. I smiled and nodded.

"I'm sorry, my mind was somewhere else entirely. It's really interesting. I guess the short answer is *yes*, it's working, but I do feel I've a lot to learn. Confidence, for example. It's essential to telling a story. If you want the story to be convincing, you have to tell it with conviction. And, as we have discussed, the salesperson is primarily selling his or herself."

"That's all good." Jack nodded.

"And do you think your approach has changed?"

"I'm finding that I'm focusing on presenting myself as well as the product. If prospects remember their impression of me, they will remember who to go to when they want to find out more. If they just remember the product without remembering me, that's not much use to me."

I paused for a moment. I couldn't very well say that talking to him had made the difference. Aside from sounding like a fawning fan, it wasn't actually the answer.

"I think there are two things that are working for me the most. First of all, removing what I want to say from one context and putting it into another. That way, the focus is all on the overall point I'm trying to make, not the actual circumstances of the deal."

He nodded in agreement.

"It's like when a photographer uses a 'cyc'—that curved white background," he said, indicating a right-angled curve with his napkin.

"Everything they photograph in front of it is pin-sharp and clear. Every detail is visible because there are no distractions. In our case, we need the story backdrop to give a context in which the action can take place. By making it alien, surreal, or fantastic, we remind the listener that the part at the centre is the bit they need to focus on."

"That's exactly it," I replied. There was a brief pause.

"And the second thing?" he asked. I had to think for a moment, and then I picked up my own thread and continued.

"The second thing I call the Polo-mint approach. Perhaps you don't know Polo mints, but they're shaped like Life Savers with a hole in the middle."

He nodded, so I went on.

"This is where you talk around the subject. Not avoiding it—far from it—but drawing its shape with topics that surround it. So, if I'm selling water pumps, I don't actually talk about water pumps. I talk about flooding, leaking pipes, basements, cellars below the water table, Hurricane Sandy, loss of business, droughts, and pipework—anything that relates to the customer's business and the customer's pain rather than my product. My product may be the ultimate answer, but it's not the question."

"I like it!" He laughed. "Make your solution the 'elephant in the room.'"

As he said this, a large white plate emerged over his shoulder, proffered by a very friendly and efficient staff member who knew all about courtesy and welcome but not a lot about the art of serving. Three noses were hit by unseen plates and one coffee cup—as yet empty—was knocked to the floor. Bit by bit and one by one, we all had our feasts before us.

"So," Jack began, chewing his way through a bacon rind.

"What sort of prospects have you been applying this new approach to?"

I went on to tell him about Alf, Henrik, and Charles. In each case I weighed up the pros and cons of the individuals as prospects and what I believed my challenges to be. I found myself recounting the details of my meeting with Alf, Karl, and Dominic on the Thursday following my commando operation at the Chamber of Commerce function.

As is often the case, the breakfast took less time to eat than it did to prepare. Soon the table was a mess of empty plates, half-finished slices of toast, and empty coffee cups. As we got up and stretched, the beach presented itself through the windows, and there were three simultaneous suggestions that we take a walk before getting back on the bikes.

Jack and I continued our conversation as we ambled slowly across the sand. Soon we had caught up with the others, who were lined up along the shore skimming stones. As I've always told my kids, it's great to be a boy. I'm sure it's great being a girl too, but it's not something I'm familiar with. I love the fact that whether we're computer programmers, psychiatrists, mechanics, or dancers, we are still in touch with the same things that gave us a thrill when we were ten—including our fanatical, infantile, competitive streaks. It's a sandy beach for the most part, so pebbles were few and far between, but we found them. For a good ten minutes we competed. The record was seven skims from Brian.

It seemed a long time since that peacock had blasted us out of our beds. I looked at my watch and saw that it was now 9:30 a.m. Others noticed me looking, and soon we were all agreed that we should be straddling our bikes and getting out of town.

When we got back to the bikes, a crowd of kids, surfers, and envious middle-aged men was gathered around them, getting as close to the machines as they could without touching, lest they get burned, bitten, or stung. I'll admit I enjoy this bit. There was a couple with their five or six-year-old son nearby. I signaled to the guy to put the kid up on the bike so he could take a photo. He did, much to the mother's feigned disgust. After a couple of minutes of answering ill-informed questions asked by guys who would have hopped on as pillion riders at the drop of a hat, we were off.

The plan was to head across country to Dunmore East in County Waterford, spend the night there, and then return to Dublin the following day. It's an unusual journey for me. In my experience, people tend to explore Ireland—or wherever it is they hail from—in a radial way out of their home area, but I was looking forward to travelling around the rim rather than down one of the spokes, if that makes sense. And despite any impression you might get from a map, it's a long ride along byroads and B roads. At this rate, it would be well into evening by the time we reached our destination.

152

We pulled out onto the road, each of us with what I call a "dot-to-dot" strapped to our tanks—a list of towns to head for along the way. *Get to one, seek the next, get to one, seek the next*—our first town being Listowel.

Back out on the road, it took me a while to get into my comfortable think zone. There was a lot more navigation to be done on this journey than on our main road excursions, so instead of the luxurious meditation of semi-autopilot, I was actually going to have to look where I was going and read the road signs. After half an hour or so, I got into the rhythm of it.

I wondered what words of wisdom Jack would have to offer regarding my other two prospects. Would my duck-shooting connections lead to anything with Henrik? What would my next step be with Charles Canterbury? I'll be honest with you, he did not strike me as Mr. Personality. One piece of advice I've drummed into anyone I've trained is this: Don't get caught up on liking someone. The trouble is that common interests and common sense of humor are blind alleys from a sales point of view. You end up focusing on the wrong people and the wrong deals.

A friend of mine once told me of how he had worked as a waiter at a surf resort while he was a student. It was a busy place, but a mom-and-pop outfit. It was cheap enough to attract the young surfers, but it was conventional and unthreatening enough for the older people to feel at home in it.

He was very happy with the tips he'd been making, especially as the basic pay wasn't much. After a month or so, he got talking to the other waiter—also a student—about tips.

"Terrible, aren't they?" his colleague had said.

"I dunno. How much do you expect to make?" said my friend, not wanting to show his hand.

"Last place I worked I was making five or six dollars a night, easy. Last night, I made one dollar. Just one dollar."

My friend bought his colleague a beer and changed the subject. Fast. Over the previous six weeks, he had been making an average of thirty dollars a night. He hadn't thought about it; he just thought people were generous. He gave the same attention, the same service, and the same smile to every table. Some left generous tips and some left none.

"To quote Karl Marx," he had said, "'From each according to their ability, to each according to his need.'"

Over the following week, he observed his colleague in action. When taking or delivering an order to an elderly couple, he would be efficient and courteous but brusque. When he was taking or delivering an order to a table surfers, however, he couldn't do enough. He would linger and joke with them, and when it came to paying the bill, he would draw up a chair and go through the whole thing. They were his peers, they were cool, and he had a lot in common with them—including the fact that they were broke.

My friend, on the other hand, was being adopted by old ladies who wanted to bring him home and feed him. He was giving joy and attention to old men who lived alone and for whom a meal in the corner café was the high point of their day. Individually, they weren't leaving him vast sums, but when added up at the end of the day, they made a tidy sum.

The moral of the story is, if you think someone is going to be a lifelong friend, get business out of the way first. And that includes corporate events. You can be golf partners with a prospect for a day and be photographed holding the cup above your heads in the national media. It doesn't make you best friends. If you're even thinking about friendship in a business deal, you're focusing on the wrong thing. Friendship will come later, when you both look back nostalgically on what a great day it was."

I laughed to myself as I remembered this anecdote, wondering how long it would be before I altered it, resized it, and pulled it out in some presentation or other. Mind you, I found it hard to imagine telling prospects I didn't want to be their friends. There aren't many circumstances in which that would seem appropriate.

I was interested in what Jack had said about different kinds of stories. There were stories for positioning yourself; stories for helping to build rapport and show what sort of a person you were; stories to show a prospect you understood their business, need, or pain; and stories that helped move negotiations forward when nobody's quite sure where to go next. Then there are leverage stories—the variety I had unknowingly performed so well with Alf. I'm sure there are other kinds, but those are the ones I'd gleaned from what Jack had said on the beach.

I asked myself what position my products and I were in. Were we a David to the multinational Goliath? (Remember, folks, David won!) Were we the Magnificent Seven—ready to come in to protect your company from marauders? Were we peacemakers—the ones who bring a solution that pleases the optimum amount of people in the least amount of time? It might seem flippant to think about your business in these terms, but at the end of the day your business has to represent something; it has to know where it sits in the market, and you have to be confident of why your potential customers might want you. And when I say "where your product sits in the market," I don't just mean price. There may be people in your market who are consciously targeting a specific group and are no threat to you.

My friend Dave works in marketing. That is, if you can call it work and keep a straight face...Hey, I'm in sales, he's in marketing, we rub each other up—it's what we do. Anyway, he talks about "positioning." Before he'll let a client put a label on their jar—never mind put out a commercial or a press release—he puts them through the wringer to establish their position: their position in relation to their competitors, their position in the consumer's life, and their position in retailers' profit hierarchy. He calls it "interrogating the brand" or some such phrase dreamed up by men in sharp suits, and the interrogation goes something like this:

Who are you selling to?

What are you selling them?

Why would they want it?

What are they using now instead of your product?

What makes your product better than that?

How have they lived this long without your product?

Why would they choose it over all the alternatives?

When you're finished, you end up with a positioning statement, something like:

"For all non-macrobiotic vegetarians, Bob's Beans offers the ideal high-protein, low-calorie main meal solution, because it's versatile, natural, nutritious, and affordable."

When he explained this process to me over a few beers, in yet another futile attempt to explain to me how his company managed to command such enormous fees, I thought he was talking a lot of hokum. It's only now, seeing how I must present my products and myself, that I realize we're both telling stories. As a person, I can change how I present myself, and in most cases, I can explain myself to people if they don't understand something I've said. A product sitting on a supermarket shelf can't enter into a dialogue—it has to have its story straight from the get-go.

I made a mental note to myself to apologize to Dave. The scales had fallen from my eyes. Now I realized that I actually had to put a positioning around myself before I could coherently put myself in front of a prospect.

The route cross-country was probably the most complex route I'd done with the club. As anyone who has tried driving or cycling in Ireland will tell you, signposting is not great, and with our refusal to stoop to satnav usage, we were to be seen debating at a great many crossroads over the next seven hours. We could have taken more major roads by detouring north or south, but given the fact that we were all out for the ride and for the love of the road, it seemed to me more adventurous to go as the crow might have flown.

156

I thought a great deal about many things during our journey. I noted places I'd like to come back to and explore but probably never would. I thought about the kids: their growth, their schooling, and their plans. I thought about golf and how much less I'd played since I got the Harley. The fact is, I don't miss it. There's no contest between eighteen holes and the open road. As you might expect after such an intense breakfast conversation, my thoughts kept coming back to storytelling in general and my current prospect interaction in particular.

The stories I had used so far had worked well and had been appropriate in the contexts I'd used them. In fact, I was quite pleased with myself, but I was still only at the beginner's level. If I wanted to use the power of stories to its best advantage, I would have to be able to draw on a pool of anecdotes, stories, fables, parables, jokes, and histories that would support anything from general relationship building and positioning to overcoming objections and leveraging. We had another day left of this ride-out, and I was determined to corner Jack once more before we reached home to get a bit more out of him about story structure.

Even though it was June and close to the longest day of the year, the sun was definitely descending as I saw the sea appear over the brow of the hill and the village of Dunmore East reveal itself. The countryside was quiet as the sound of my Harley cut a swathe between the hedges. I passed a distinctly South American-looking church in the middle of nowhere, which brought back that "spaghetti western" feeling I'd had a couple of times riding through villages. Across the breadth of the bay they call Waterford Harbor, I could see what I took to be Hook Lighthouse, which, along with Crooke Head further west, gave rise to the expression "By Hook or by Crooke." That was another place I decided I'd have to visit someday. It's the oldest functioning lighthouse in the world; the building itself is eight hundred years old. I coasted down the hill for the last few miles into the village. We were to meet at the Strand Inn before heading out to the campsite. Compared to the last time we camped, this was heavenly—a beautiful sunny day with the promise of a dry, windless night.

The engine sounds from my Harley were magnified as I rode between the walls of houses, causing one or two curtains to twitch in curiosity. My instructions were to keep riding until I saw the slipway down to the beach. Sure enough, there was the Strand Inn with one noble, weathered, and familiar hawg parked outside it. Silhouetted against the blue evening sky, an equally familiar figure sat on the sea wall looking out towards Hook Head. I switched off my engine, put the bike on its stand, and without turning round, he said, "Hey, Seb, what's the story?

ELEVATOR PITCHES VS. TOP STORIES

If you want to get to the top, you have to learn to push the right buttons

> "Do you know the difference between an elevator pitch and a movie pitch? Jack asked.
>
> "No," I replied. "I could guess, but somehow I don't think I'd come up with the answer you're looking for."
>
> "An elevator pitch can last twenty-five, fifty, even seventy storeys. A movie pitch is twenty-five words or less."

That got me thinking. The stories we read our children are no differently constructed than those we read as adults; the differences are merely the topics, the language, and the duration. In pondering the movie pitch as a tool to convey a movie in twenty-five words, I got to thinking. Once you have your story distilled into something that short, you can do what you like with it. Take the musical *West Side Story*, one of the only musicals I'll admit to having watched and enjoyed. It's a lift of Shakespeare's *Romeo and Juliet* from Renaissance Verona to 1950s New York—with some songs added in. And what are those twenty-five words?

"Lovers defy their feuding families. To avoid an arranged marriage, Juliet drinks potion. Thinking she's dead, Romeo commits suicide. She wakes, finds him, and does the same."

And there you have a portable story that can travel through time and space and be dressed according to your needs.

When I look back on the stories I used to read to the kids when they were small, there were the greats—the ones I had loved—and in some cases, my parents had loved them, too. *Winnie the Pooh, Charlie and the Chocolate Factory,* even *Wind in the Willows.* The genius behind those stories is that they appeal to adults and to kids. Everybody wins. The adult is interested enough to read with enthusiasm, and the child enjoys the story and the telling. But what is it that makes these stories so attractive? Is there a structure to them that locks the reader or listener in from the first sentence? Is there a particular rhythm? Is it the characters, the words, or the setting? Could it be the anticipation of knowing there is a twist in the tale just around the corner? All of this had been going through my mind since Jack's question, as I stared out towards the distant black-and-white stripes of Hook Lighthouse and the long, flat strip of Hook Head, interrupted by only one large house and one lonely tree, both clearly visible past what must have been six or seven miles of sea.

My mind came back across the water to Jack and what he had said. We were sitting on a long sea wall, at the head of a small bay, with a beach about twenty feet below us and another to our left, about half a mile over some rocks. Like the first time we'd met, Jack had arrived at the destination first and I had come along second. The bar we were all to meet in was to our left; it was built right up to the sea wall.

"So, what has you asking me riddles about about movie pitches and elevator pitches?" I asked.

"Well, a few reasons, really. First off, I reckon pitching movies to Hollywood producers is about the purest use of a story in selling. You are literally trying to engage their interest and open their wallets with a story. No software package, no car, no insurance policy—just a story.

"This is why we really have to look at how successful movies tell their stories: to learn how we can create stories that will open hearts, minds, and wallets."

I hadn't thought of that before. When a writer pitches a movie in Hollywood, he uses the encapsulated story to sell that same story on a much grander scale. As if reading my mind, Jack continued.

"The movie director John Boorman once described the process as 'turning money into light' because, in the Hollywood scenario, you're using twenty-five words to secure twenty-five-million dollars to create a lot of flickering light on a screen. If they can do that with twenty-five words, you can sell your software."

I nodded. It was funny to think of people committing millions of dollars to a project on the basis of twenty-five words. Obviously, there was much more to the process, but his point was very valid.

"You said there were a few reasons you were talking about movie pitches for selling. What were the others?" I asked.

He held a cupped hand face up and pointed the finger of his other hand into it.

"The story fits in the palm of your hand. It doesn't take up any space in your mind, in your hard drive, or in your notebook. With the twenty-five word summary, you have what you need. Better still, the fact that it lacks detail means you can adapt it by adding details to suit your specific situation. Once a story contains the bare essentials, it can be reshaped and resized to fit whatever the situation calls for."

This brought me back to my earlier reverie. "Like *West Side Story*, which was basically *Romeo and Juliet*."

"That's right," he said enthusiastically. "If there's an important message in a story, you might find today's kids listening better to a story about the Cripps and the Bloods in twenty-first century Los Angeles than to a tale about the Montagues and the Capulets in sixteenth-century Verona.

"There are plenty of other examples. *Apocalypse Now*, the archetypal Vietnam movie, is based on *Heart of Darkness*, Joseph Conrad's novel set in nineteenth-century Congo."

I hadn't realised that, and I resisted the temptation to stray into a conversation about *Apocalypse Now* in favour of staying with the point. I was conscious that the others would be with us soon, and the subject would be lost among the inevitable stories and anecdotes of the road trip, which, after all, was why we were all here.

"OK, with you so far," I began. "But can you know when a story has everything it needs? How can you be sure when you're creating a story that it will fold like a deckchair and fit neatly into the twenty-five words without collapsing like a house of cards?"

He nodded and smiled in that way schoolteachers do when they are about to tell you something you should already know.

"Type and structure, my friend, type and structure. I told you about the structure of a story, didn't I? It's like giving someone directions on a journey: you start with your hero, heroine, or anti-hero and how and where they are at the beginning. The 'setting,' in other words.

"For example, 'Jack and his mother were very poor and had no food.'

"That's the status quo, if you will. Leave that as it is and they may die of hunger, but it's not much of a children's story. We need something to change. A complication, a turning point:

"'Mom tells Jack he'll have to take Bessie to the market and sell her so they can have money to buy food.'

"As with many stories, the complication, or turning point, is a biggie in the *Jack and the Beanstalk* story. If he'd just brought the money home there wouldn't have been a complication, and we wouldn't have had a story. But he trades Bessie for some magic beans, Mom throws the beans out the window, we have a beanstalk, a giant, and yadda, yadda, yadda..."

It was kind of funny watching this bearded frontiersman, sitting with his zip-back leather biking boots dangling off a wall, analyse a fairy tale. He looked so serious that I nearly broke into a fit of laughter. I thought I'd stiffle the urge with a well-placed question.

"That's pretty much the story done," I said. "Seems to me that it's one big complication. All that fee-fi-fo-fum stuff, golden eggs, talking harps..."

"Sure, you can say that. But if that was the whole story, it would mean leaving Jack up in the cloud castle, hiding from the giant. A three-year-old could tell you that the story isn't over until the giant's dead, don't you think?"

He looked at me expectantly, as if I could contradict him. I couldn't.

"If it's to be a story—a *satisfying* story—it must have a resolution, or, if you want to be fancy, a *denouement*. Denouement means 'untying' or 'untangling' in French, which is kind of funny, because in English we'd call it 'tying up loose ends.'

"Anyways, what happens to Jack? He hightails it down that stalk, grabs an axe, and cuts the stalk down, conveniently killing the giant in the process.

"So, for Jack and his mom it's over. Done deal. Not only are they safe, with food in the larder, Jack has learned a valuable lesson and proved himself as a man. In the old stories, when a guy killed someone, he somehow seemed to qualify as a man.

"So, if you want to know a story's value, you subtract the setting from the resolution. You look at the change that's taken place in the subject's life—hero, heroine, or anti-hero—and that's the story's worth. So whether it's a twenty-five-word pitch or a seventy-storey elevator pitch, apply the same logic."

Yes, it made sense, but when I hear things presented to me as theory or analysis, they always come across too tidy for my liking. It's all too neat. I remember this from stuff I learned in school: I'd say to myself, *that's great*, and then I'd go and apply it in the real world and find out it wasn't all that simple. When I was sixteen, my parents let me decorate my room. There was this cool wallpaper I wanted. Treating me like an adult, they gave me a budget and told me to get the supplies myself. Pencil behind my ear, steel measuring tape in hand, and geometry class top of mind, I set about measuring the amount of wallpaper I required. Only then did I see my bedroom walls for what they were: a mass of slopes, angles, fitted cupboards, ventilation pipes, dado rails, skirtings, architraves, angles, twists, and corners that would have put Pythagoras, Archimedes, and Einstein in a spin.

"OK," I said, "that's very neat and tidy. I can see how an Aesop's Fable can have a handy, measurable transition. *The Tortoise and the Hare* has a maxim of 'Slow and steady wins the race' because that's what the protagonists learned. In *The Boy Who Cried Wolf*, we learn that if you abuse people's good will, that good will dries up. But those stories were clearly written to give us lessons, messages, or 'transitions.' Where in the heck is the message or transition in *Jack and the Beanstalk*?"

164

He smiled. It wasn't the schoolteacher smile this time. Oh no. This time—to my satisfaction, I'll admit—it looked like it was a "you got me there" sort of a smile.

"Well, I guess we're reading that story to our kids as simple bedtime entertainment, but those stories originally had a purpose. *Jack and the Beanstalk* goes way back in England, and some say it came over to England with the Vikings, which would make it very old indeed. But like I said, Jack killed a guy, which in Viking culture would have made him a man. And killing a giant pretty much confers 'legend' status on a man. But joking aside, the serious answer to your question is that Jack transforms from an awkward adolescent, to capable, coping adult. It could be called *How Jack Became a Man* or *Jack Steps Up to the Plate*.

"Now, can you picture Viking Captain Magnus telling his baby heir Erik a bedtime story? What thoughts does he want his little Valhalla-bound offspring to take with him to dreamland? Simple. He's teaching the future warrior that actions have consequences, and consequences require reactions."

I laughed and shook my head.

"Oooh, you're good. You're very good! I don't want to admit it, but you are very good. And actually, you've highlighted another thing about stories. They can simply illustrate, demonstrate, or clarify a point, but they also convey important lessons. That action-re-action-consequence lesson you mention has been learned the hard way by many a kid, with smack around the ear. A story is the spoon full of sugar that helps the medicine go down."

He nodded. I went on.

"But what I want to know, Jack, my friend," I said with tongue in cheek, "What sort of sales pitch was it that got Jack to buy the beans in the first place?"

As we laughed, we heard the sound of bikes behind us, their engines amplified by the walls of the houses as they entered the street. I was very hungry, and sitting outside a bar in a very beautiful place with such a spectacular view somehow didn't seem right without a beer. At the same time, I was disappointed that our conversation was coming to an end. Jack was good company. Yes, I was learning a lot of facts and theories from him, but more than that, I was getting extra-large portions of that well-known dish called "food for thought."

We jumped down off the wall to greet the guys. As we did so, I said:

"OK, you're off the hook for now, my friend, but we're not finished. We've done structure—hero, setting, complication, and resolution—but you also mentioned 'type.' I'd really like to hear about that."

"Sure thing," he replied.

It was only then that I looked at my watch and saw the time. It was seven o'clock, and we'd been on the road since 9:30 a.m. Nine and a half hours—though obviously not all of it was riding. An hour of it had been spent at another roadside pub, where we'd sat in the sun and ate our respective weights in calories. A couple of brief rest stops too, of course, but as I had expected, we spent a great deal of time standing at crossroads scratching our heads. Signposts are—and I'll be polite about this—a "challenge" in this part of the world. Combine that with our steadfast refusal to bow to cowardly, cop-out technology like a satnav, and you have a whole lot of lost men in leather. Let's face it, it's about what we do and why we do it. Where else in our lives can we feel as if we're living on our wits without some form of constraint or restriction getting in our way?

But here we all were, eight guys with eight appetites and eight thirsts, not to mention four tents that had to be pitched before either of them could be sated or slaked. The campsite was, according to the directions I'd downloaded off the web, up the hill and straight on for about a mile. It wasn't actually a campsite, to be honest, it was a bit of land another club member

166

had organised for us. It certainly seemed handy to the village. We straddled our bikes and motored slowly up the hill, each of us gasping at the beautiful view of the view which, as we went up the hill, revealled more of the extraordinary red stone cliffs and golden beaches. We reached a crossroads with a church where Cormac, who was in the lead, signalled to me to come to the front, as I was the one who knew where we were going.

We found the place all right. There was a rather run-down cottage with a garden around it. The garden was perfect for camping in, and we had a key to the cottage, so we had a bathroom. One look inside the place and I was happy I was camping, not staying inside. Anyway, with the efficiency that only determined men with big appetites can muster, we parked the bikes, pitched camp, removed our leathers, and sauntered down the hill in civilian clothing.

While we knew there was plenty more of the village to explore, there was no debate about it. We all headed back to the inn where we'd met. We walked down the road to the church, crossed the junction, and from there the sea unfolded before us. There was a collective intake of breath. The contrast of cobalt water and emerald grass separated by rust-coloured cliffs and golden sand was awe inspiring. As we walked downhill with the road to our left, a three-foot wall on our right—like a banister rail—was all that stood between us and a fifty-foot drop to the beach. Of course, that drop reduced as we went down the hill, but a glance at my comrades told me that none of them were watching where they were going. All eyes were on the view. What is it about views that captivates us? Whether it is beautiful scenery, an attractive woman, or a work of art, all of us are capable of entering a semidaze, our jaws dragging on the ground. I suppose that's why appearances are so important. If a Ferrari had the same engineering in a less pleasing bodywork, it would be much harder to sell.

On reaching the inn, the full force of our appetites struck us like a gong. It was well after eight o'clock when we were faced with the choice of an elegant seafood restaurant or a burger-and-steak bar. Again, there was no debate; let's face it, fancy restaurants don't carry much biker cred. In we strode to the burger joint, making a beeline for a good-sized nook in the corner of the cosy seaside bar. There were specimen fish in glass cases, fishing nets strewn hither and yon, and an anchor propped up in a corner. Menus were scanned with military speed and efficiency, and an order, probably constituting half a cow in burger and steak meat, went to the kitchen, accompanied by an order for the requisite quantity of beer.

There followed the collective sigh of a team relaxing after accomplishing a vital task. There was some good banter about the various experiences had on the road, either collectively or individually. As I had predicted, Max the Mechanic had spent an hour tweaking Gordon's bike to sort out an oil leak. I guess that's the price you pay for riding a classic bike…cool comes at a price. We tease Bertrand that his bike has a mind of its own, and it didn't disappoint us. He took a wrong turn that led to a forty-mile detour and a forced cup of tea at a farmhouse where he had asked directions. Otherwise, it was the usual exchange about scenery, sights along the way, and a litany of complaints about bad driving from our four-wheeled friends. The food began to arrive, a fleet of starch-and-protein-laden flying saucers hovering above our heads on the upraised palms of the waitstaff. As we each identified ourselves as "rare," "blue cheese," "with bacon," and so on, our plate would float to a precise landing on the placemat in front of us. We raised our black-and-amber pint glasses to toast Messrs. Harley and Davidson and the glories of the road. Then we began to eat.

The almost sacred pause in conversation lasted a couple of minutes as we savoured our first few mouthfuls. The food began to go to work. Brian broke the silence, addressing me and Jack, who was sitting beside me.

"So, are you two still talking fairy tales?"

We laughed. His words were flippant, but I could see from his face he was ready to continue the discussion we'd had outside the pub.

"I guess you could say we are," Jack answered. "But like everyone, we're looking for that elusive happy ending."

"But seriously," Brian said, his talent as a performer actually convincing us that he was about to say something serious. "I have a story for you."

"Well, let's have it," said Jack, expressionless and motionless.

"This actually happened in a suburb of Dublin, just a couple of weeks ago," Brian began, underlining the seriousness of whatever it was he was going to tell us. "A ten-year-old girl was walking home alone from school one day. It was a route she walked everyday; she knew people along the way, and she was a familiar face to the shopkeepers and locals in the area. A big guy on a large black motorcycle was seen to pull up alongside her, going just fast enough to stay upright but slow enough to keep pace with her. After following her in silence for a few hundred feet, he turned his head, flicked up his visor, and said to the little girl, 'Hey there, do you want to go for a ride?'

"'No!' she replied, just as her mother had schooled her.

"She kept on walking. But the motorcyclist persisted. After another few hundred feet, he zipped a bit ahead of her, paused the bike, and faced her, saying, 'I will give you ten euro if you hop on the back.'

"'I said no!' the brave little girl said, as she began to scurry down the footpath at speed. But it only took a twist of the wrist for the motorcyclist to catch up and overtake her again. Notwithstanding the fact that his face was bunched up and he had pouched cheeks, he looked intimidating in the full-face helmet and black leather gear.

"There was menace in the air as he said, 'I'm feeling generous today! I'll give you twenty bucks and a big bag of candy if you will just hop on the back of my bike and go for a ride with me.'

"The courageous little girl stopped in her tracks. She turned and faced the biker, fists on her hips and legs akimbo. Glaring at him, she screamed out at the top of her voice so all the passers-by would hear her. 'Look, Dad, you're the one who bought the Honda instead of the Harley! So ride it by yourself!'"

The table erupted. Brian had timed and measured every phrase, building the tension in such a way that, even though we knew it had to be a gag, the punchline had the power and surprise of Muhammad Ali in his prime. When the laughter settled, I realised Brian's interest in stories wasn't superficial.

"I've been thinking about stories a good bit," he said. "Is it true that there's a limited amount of story types out there? I read somewhere that there are, literally, only seven story types and that you can take any story you like and break it down into one of those seven."

"You mean like 'Boy meets girl, girl likes boy, they live happily ever after' or 'Boy meets girl, girl doesn't like boy, boy joins a monastery'—that kind of thing?" I asked.

"That kind of thing, yeah. I think the number was seven." Brian took another corner of steak, closing his eyes in delight.

"Why don't we look it up." I took out my phone and searched, 'How many types of story are there?'

I was surprised at the search results. There were a lot of sites covering the subject, and obviously, the three of us weren't the only ones posing the question. In a way, I regretted doing the search, because not only was it a bit antisocial, I also wanted to do some more damage to my burger.

"OK," I began. "There's a whole heap of stuff here, but this one looks the most interesting: 'The Basic Plots in Literature.' In a nutshell, it says that it's a pretty futile question—but if you want an answer, there are different opinions. Some say there's only one plot: conflict. That theory claims that all stories are built around conflict.

"Then there are others who say there are three, seven—that's your buddy, Brian—twenty, or thirty-six plots. The three option is bizarre—it's just 'happy ending, unhappy ending,' and 'literary ending.'

Jack had been very quiet; he was making his way slowly but surely through a steak about the size of a tennis racket. I got to thinking of the breakfast we had eaten that morning and reckoned that even if we'd cycled the distance on an actual pedal bicycle, we wouldn't have burned up that much food. Jack put his knife and fork down—something I realised none of us had done so far during the meal, such was our hunger.

"The thing is," Jack said, "all of that might tell you what a story is about—where it's set and who's in it—but it doesn't really tell you the takeaway. Not how I see it, anyway. To a certain degree, I'd go along with him saying all stories are about conflict, because at some point in any functioning story, there has to be a change, a contrast, a turning point which suggests a change from one reality or realisation to another. That's how we get a resolution."

"Well, Jack, I think this neatly takes us to where we left off on the wall out there. How many types of story do you reckon there are?" I asked.

"Well, I can't speak for literature, philosophy, or religion stories, but I can speak for selling stories. In my book, there are three primary areas where I can apply stories to improve my business relationships: one, to make a personal connection with the other person—or *prospect*, to use sales language; two, to establish the relevance of my business to their business or situation; and three, to adjust attitudes by getting rid of the negative preconceptions people might have about me or what I'm offering."

As Jack listed off these scenarios, I realised that they were not exclusive to selling. I smiled to myself. All three are techniques guys instinctively use when trying to attract a woman's attention – which I guess is a form of selling too. We try to make a connection by casually bumping into her, holding a door open, or commenting on the weather. We try to be relevant by identifying common interests or experiences. Then we endeavour to adjust her attitude to a point where she sees us as being worthy of a date. I thought about sharing this pearl of wisdom, but then thought better of it. Instead, I asked him to give us a couple of illustrations. Jack went on.

> "In a business context, we regularly have to lumber into other people's lives—people with whom we have no interests in common and no experiences in common—superficially, at least. If we want to make an impression and earn trust, we have to make connections with people."

Cormac nodded.

> "I remember noticing when I first began working that when guys— clients, customers, or whoever—had meetings, went for coffee, or had a sandwich, conversation would always be about football or golf. Or it if was a bar or cafe, there might be a comment or two on the waitress. I used to think that was so shallow or crass, but I guess sport and women are common ground and allow a rudimentry connection, at least."

> "That wasn't quite what I had in mind," Jack smiled, "but I guess you're right, up to a point. I'm talking about more key things about yourself—things that will impact directly on the deal you hope to strike. Things with more impact and importance than sex and soccer!"

> "And what could possibly be more important than those two?" Cormac said with mock indignation. There was laughter.

"OK, let's say I tell a story of how I messed up one time. That would communicate to my prospect that I don't hide from my mistakes; I learn from them. So long as I'm careful to make it clear that I don't mess up often, it helps him to see me as more human and less like the sales stereotype.

"It's important to be fresh and original with these kind of stories. If you trot out the same one each time, it's going to sound more fake in each different context. That being said, I have a couple of stock stories I pull out and adapt. There's the time I got halfway through a sales process on a $1 million sale and then told the prospect it wasn't for him. That was on 15-percent commission, so it was a sacrifice. Darned near lost me my job, too, when my boss heard, but it was the right thing to do. I ended up making a $4 million sale to the same guy two years later! Then there's the time a European client paid the dollar figure in euro, which meant an overspend of about $20,000. I made sure they got a rebate.

"They don't have to be 'good boy scout' stories, either—just stories that help convey something of your character and make-up. And so long as they have a basis in fact and you can tell them convincingly, stories like these can really bed down your relationship with a prospect."

I thought this was all well and good, but how could you build up a stock of stories that help make personal connections with people you hadn't met yet? I had to ask.

"OK, Jack, I can see the value in this," I said. "But how can you prepare for that? How can you anticipate what sort of connections you're going to make or which aspects of your personality you'll want to showcase?"

"Didn't say it was easy," he replied sardonically. "I guess the best way is, every now and again, to go over your past experiences and try to come up with things that would have worked in previous situations. There's only so many ways the dice roll in the sales game."

Fair answer, I thought. Jack went on to explain how stories can help establish the relevance or context of you or your product to a prospect's business.

"The odds are that by the time you find yourself in a sales discussion, you've established what your customer's discomfort is—what problem they need solved. Hopefully, you've also explained what it is you're selling. Now you need something to bring the two together—something that establishes the relevance your product has to that pain or discomfort. To put it another way, this is your chance to answer their question, 'Why should I care about you and what you have to sell?'

"This is where stories about other similar businesses you've dealt with, in the same category as the prospect or other applications where your product has solved similar problems, come in handy. These are actually pretty vital stories, because people don't buy facts alone—they buy contexts. That's why so many commercials and advertisements use customer stories. Yes, your website, your brochure, and your sales spiel all lay out the facts, but if they could actually sell stuff on their own, the sales guy would be out of a job. The context story, the story that establishes relevance, is the story that invites your prospect in the door and sets him down beside the fire with a nice cup of java. It's the story that allows you to tell the sales story. It's the story that says, 'Are you sitting comfortably? Well now, I'll begin.'"

I thought back on the hundreds of salesman jokes I've heard. The advertising guys get called liars and the sales guys get called thieves, but in what Jack had said I heard a truth I hadn't really been aware of. The salesperson is a catalyst that brings about the sales response. The prospect has a need, and in a great many cases, he or she could go out, do a bit of research, and find the answer they want—the way we would if we were buying a low-ticket item like a stapler or a kettle. Once the product or service gets to be higher in value, however, we need to see a person alongside the item who can act as a lightning rod to draw away our doubts and an ally to support us in our decision. A salesperson is therefore like a midwife providing Lamaze training for the prospect. And with that rather uncomfortable image lingering in my mind, Jack began discussing his third story type.

"The third type of story I like to call 'the Attitude Adjustor,'" he said with a malevolent grin. "Yup, sounds violent, doesn't it! If you get a feeling that your prospect has an inaccurate perception of you or the relevance of what you do, telling a story can turn this perception on its head. Perhaps you feel they think you're too old-fashioned, too small, too large, too exotic, too expensive, too arrogant, or too modest.

"He might not have been my favorite politician, but this response from Ronald Reagan gets me every time. During the 1984 candidate debates, somebody asked if, as a seventy-three-year-old, he was too old to be president. He responded by saying, 'I will not make age an issue of this campaign. I am not going to exploit, for political purposes, my opponent's youth and inexperience.' Brilliant. Now, you might argue that that's not a story, it's at best an anecdote. No matter. I'm not telling you to read them bedtime stories to lull them into submission, I'm telling you to use sharp, pithy communications to modify how you and your product are perceived."

Jack paused and took a long overdue pull on his beer.

"If someone has the wrong idea about you," he went on, "you're not going to correct it by simply saying, 'Hey, you've got the wrong idea about me.' You have to demonstrate it in some way. If they see you as more expensive than a competitor whose product is unstable, you can't just say, 'Their product is unstable.' If you do that, you might as well have said, 'Our product is better, so there! Ya boo sucks!' You have to demonstrate and illustrate these things. Here's a true story. I used to do work with a company that makes stairlifts for people who find the stairs difficult. They made no pretence of being cheap, but they did talk about quality and reliability. They were very proud of how few calls they got on their 24/7, 365 days a year service-and-repair hotline. They got few calls because there were few breakdowns. In fact, they said, the majority of the calls they got were from prospects they had visited and quoted but who had gone with a cheaper provider instead. Now, with installation and payment complete, those companies that got the contracts either weren't answering service calls or were quoting prohibitive call-out charges. In other words, these prospects calling were people who wished they had paid more to get the best.

"Another attitude-adjustor story is one that shows your product as the choice for a more demanding situation or a highly admired business. One of the most bizarre stories I've heard was about a global brand of infant disinfectant, designed for soaking diapers, selling itself to restaurants for cleaning their surfaces. And who can argue with that? If it's gentle enough and strong enough to keep babies safe, it sounds ideal for restaurants. I'm still not sure if I like the idea of seeing diaper-soaking solution in a restaurant kitchen!

"I guess I've taken you through my key story types. Maybe there are thirty-six different kinds of story in the literary world, but to get yourself through business and sales, I guarantee my three will do the trick. You can make 'em first-person stories that make out they actually happened to you, but if you do, mind you don't set yourself any traps. Or you can make them into third-person stories—sometimes that's safer. You know the sort of thing: 'I knew a guy who met someone who told him about a woman whose husband once bought a bicycle...' That kinda stuff."

"I wonder how important it is for a story to be true for it to get its message through?" Brian said. "Just because something didn't happen doesn't make the story a lie. And let's be honest, telling a bit of a yarn, or embellishing a story, can be an awful lot more interesting than a catalogue of dry facts."

Brian had finished his steak. He pushed his placemat and plate in from the edge of the table, cradled the beer glass in his hand, and settled back in the bench seat. Without saying a word, his body language informed us he was about to tell a story.

"Fadó, fadó," he said, using the Irish-language version of *a long time ago*, "when the world was younger, adults were wiser, and children knew their place, there was a village on the edge of a mountain overlooking the great green plains as they stretched towards the mighty river.

"And in that village there lived two of the most beautiful young girls God had ever created or Darwin had ever have imagined. Their names were Story and Fact.

"Now Story and Fact were born on the very same day and had been bitter rivals from their early years. And though they were both un-questionably beautiful, each was determined to outdo the other by being the most popular girl in the village.

"Their friends were tired of the squabbling and bickering. One day, one of the other girls made a proposition. Story and Fact should walk through the village between noon and one o'clock on market day. Whichever girl was greeted by the most people as she passed through the market would be the winner.

"Fact won the toss and began her walk first, with head held high. She walked past the church, the marketplace, by barrow boys, shep-herds, and farmers, fishwives, tinkers, and tradesmen, but not one of them so much as tipped a hat to her. She slumped onto a bench crying tears of frustration and sorrow.

"Story then began her walk, and from her first step she was greeted by everyone she passed. Even an old blind lady selling matches greeted her as she walked by. When she reached the bench on the otherside of the market, Fact raised her bloodshot eyes and humbly said, 'Story, you win. How is it that you're so popular?'

"'We're both the same inside,' said Story compassionately.

"'Why is it everyone lights up when they see you?' Fact asked with a sniffle.

"'The trouble is," said story, 'Nobody wants to hear the naked truth.'

"'But what am I to do?' said Fact in frustration.

"'Wear this around you, my friend,' said Story, hanging a heavy cloak over the other girl's shoulders.

"'What is it?' said Fact, intrigued.

"'It's emotion. When you wear this, truth becomes interesting, facts magnetic, and stories are born.'

This was a side of Brian I'd never seen before. He had told the tale with the energy and relish of a seasoned performer. Better still, he had used a story as a perfect way to illustrate a point. While the story's conclusion wasn't scientific proof, it was a neat encapsulation of what Jack had been saying all along. If you tell it exactly the way it happened, with the ordinary days in which nothing unusual happens, the long gaps between key events, and the uninspiring, everyday dialogue of real life, the audience will fall asleep. And, if you want to be really literal about it, the real-life nanny from *The Sound of Music* probably didn't sing quite so much. At least, I hope for those around her that she didn't.

There was a growl from the chair beside me.

"Brian," Jack said, "I'm gonna use that. That's good material. Where did you hear it?"

"I've heard it from several sources," Brian replied, "We Irish have ears like vacuum cleaners when it comes to good stories and old yarns. Somebody told me once that it's a Jewish folk story, but I don't know for certain."

A few wheels were turning in my head.

"You know something?" I said. "We talk about stories as entertainment and as a tool for passing away long winter evenings. The reality is, originally all stories were working stories. A thousand years ago, people sitting around the fire telling stories probably wouldn't have wasted their breath telling stories just to make one another laugh. As Jack has told us, *Jack and the Beanstalk* came over with the Vikings, and it had a purpose. Aesop's Fables were all, by definition, hard-working stories. It probably wasn't until the likes of Shakespeare and Cervantes that stories became entertainment— and even then, there were teaching elements involved."

Alan had been listening with one ear, slowly relishing his burger too much to make any contribution beyond a nod of the head. Now he too sat back, pushed his plate forward, and moved himself away from the table's edge to leave room for his expanded waistline.

"I hear what you're saying, Seb. To my mind, that's what makes something literature. There's nothing complicated about Aesop's Fables, for example. Shakespeare's plays are the scourge of schoolkids today, but at the time they were in the language of the common man. Likewise, Charles Dickens's novels were serialised in a mass-circulation magazine—nothing highfalutin about our Charley. The reason they've lasted so long is not because there's anything essentially 'superior' about them, but because they tell us something. Good literature has a universality about it that allows it to speak truths to many people. And that's why stories can be shortened, lengthened, simplified, filmed, and made into stage plays or radio plays. Yes, a story might have been written well by its original author, but the core of a good story can be told in a few paragraphs."

Jack and I laughed simultaneously.

"That's just what we were saying before you arrived," Jack said, stroking his beard. "Whether it's a Hollywood movie pitch or an elevator pitch, you gotta be able to hold your story right here."

He cupped his hand as he had done outside on the wall and pointed down into his palm with an index finger.

There was a lull in conversation. Jack yawned. He stretched and said he was ready to hit the hay. The sun, which had been doing a swansong along the horizon, finally made its final bow and retired for the night. A look around the bar showed us it was emptying out, and we collectively decided it was time to go. The next day was a 'pottering day.' We were just a hundred miles from home, so there was time for a leisurely breakfast and a stroll around the village in the morning. We would set off around 11:30 and meet for a sandwich halfway; then it would be every man for himself on the roads to our respective homes.

We settled the bill and set off. Quiet reigned as we went up the hill. We were transfixed by the clear night sky. Being June, it had remained light until ten in the evening, but now the stars were asserting themselves, adding sparkle to the otherwise gloomy sky. The shadowy sea stretched out to the Hook Peninsula, which was now a scattered dot-to-dot puzzle of intermittent lights.

By this time we had reached the campsite and were ready for bed. It had been a long day and we were all bleary eyed. People who don't ride motorcycles have no idea how much of a physical activity it is. For one thing, the concentration involved is constant. Car drivers may kid themselves that they have enough spare concentration to dial their phone or send a one-handed text while driving, but no motorcyclist will ever tell you that. Our eyes have to be on the road constantly, scanning what's ahead, what's behind, and anticipating what other road-users may be about to do. Then there's the muscle work. There's enough clenching and loosening of the biceps, triceps, abs, and glutes to constitute a serious workout. So it didn't

180

really matter how soft the ground was or how drafty the tent, we slept the sleep of the just.

The next morning we were up and out by eight bells. No one was ready to eat just yet, having had such a large, late dinner. We elected to explore the village and its breakfast options, aiming to eat around nine thirty.

What a beautiful village it was. The bar and beach we had seen were only a fraction of the village, which spread around the edge of the bay. We took the other turn at the church and found the most amazing little harbour with a cove full of leisure boats and the main harbour ready for business with fishing boats, ice-makers, and fish processing plants. I made up my mind to come back for a weekend with the family.

As we strolled, Brian asked me a rather unexpected question.

"Seb, do you get satisfaction out of the sales process? Or is it just the actual sale that does it for you?"

"I'd have to think about that, Brian," I replied reflectively. "There's no shying away from the 'Yes!' factor—the buzz of seing a sale go over the line—but it is great working with people. No two people and no two days are the same."

I felt it was an honest if not a comprehensive answer, but there was a low, rumbling chuckle from Jack.

"I'll tell you a little story that illustrates what it's like being in sales. Mark, a guy I knew years back, was a traditional sales rep working for a local office supplies distribution company. It's the kind of stuff everybody needs but the kind of stuff that can be bought from twenty different sources, so it was very competitive— and his customers knew it.

"With a family to support, he had stayed with the same company for years, wearing out shoe leather, knocking on doors, selling copiers and accessories. As often as not, he was banging his head against the wall.

"Day in, day out, Mark called procurement managers throughout his territory on the phone and visited them at their offices, factories, clinics, surgeries, studios, or warehouses.

"One Monday morning, Mark turned up for a meeting with Mr. McDonald, the procurement manager of a large retail chain. It should have been a sizeable bit of business, but McDonald was a real pain in the ass to deal with. No matter how Mark bent over backwards, McDonald always shopped around, left Mark waiting any time he'd visit, and loved to play mind games.

"Anyway, that Monday, Mark arrived at the gate, parked his car, and headed towards Mr. McDonald's plush offices. But when he got to the lobby, he found the lift was out of order—and McDonald's office was on the fifteenth floor.

"He took a deep breath and began the climb. Arriving at the secretary's desk out of breath but with a minute to spare, he introduced himself. 'Mark Scott. I'm here to see Mr. McDonald, the procurement manager.'

"'Oh my god. I'm so sorry, didn't you hear?' she replied.

"'Hear what?' gasped Mark, still catching his breath.

"'Mr. McDonald had a massive heart attack over the weekend,' she said. 'Just dropped dead. Not a word of warning. I'm so sorry you weren't informed.'

"Mark thanked her, turned on his heels, and headed off to his next appointment.

"The next morning, Tuesday, Mark headed back to McDonald's former office. He parked his car and made his way to the fifteenth floor. He walked up to receptionist and enquired, 'Is it possible to speak with Mr. McDonald?'

"The receptionist looked at him and thought she recognized him, but she wasn't sure—it had been a busy two days. 'I'm so sorry, I'm afraid Mr. McDonald died of a massive heart attack at the weekend. He just dropped dead. Not a word of warning—just dropped. I'm really very sorry.'

"'OK,' Mark said, and the receptionist thought his expression was very strange. He turned on his heels and headed off to his next appointment.

"Wednesday morning, Mark again returned to Mr. McDonald's former office, parked his car, and made his way to the fifteenth floor. On reaching the receptionist he asked her, 'Is it possible to speak with Mr. McDonald this morning?'

"She was now certain that she recognized him. Curtly, she repeated what he had already told him twice before. 'You were here yesterday and on Monday, and as I have told you already, Mr. McDonald died at the weekend. Did you not hear me the first time?'

"'Oh, I did,' said Mark,

"'So why do you keep coming back?'

"'Because I just love hearing that the old bastard is dead,' said Mark.

I almost choked, I laughed so much. Who knew that Jack had a sense of humour?

We had breakfast in a beautiful old Victorian Hotel with views of a park and the red-cliffed coastline. Over breakfast we discussed our next trip. Shaun suggested Newgrange and Tara.

"What's in Newgrange?" asked Jack.

"Ah, you'll love it, Jack," said Alan. "It's the home of all Irish stories, and Tara is the seat of the High Kings and the Celtic heroes of yore."

"Sounds good to me," Jack said with a laugh.

It was time to sling our hooks, weigh our anchors, and hit the road. We were going to take the coast road rather than the motorway, which would bring us through all the W's first—Waterford, Wexford, and Wicklow—and finally to Dublin. I opted not to meet them at the lunchtime stopover, as I had to head home and get a few things done for the week ahead. It had been a long trip and a great trip, and I felt elated...or maybe elevated.

BIG GAME HUNTING

When prospecting be sure to get to know the characters and their roles or your story won't have a happy ending.

I enjoyed the ride home alone. The weekend had been great, but I had used up my capacity to be part of a group. Like a lot of guys, there's a bit of the loner in me, which ironically is one of the things that drew me to bikes. The autonomy, the freedom, and the ability to be spontaneous attracted me. It's a strange human foible. No matter how solitary the activity we are drawn to, we are still drawn to be with others who feel the same way, so, as a group, we can validate our love of free, solitary roaming. No, I can't explain it any better. I love being part of the group and sharing the joys of the road, but after two days I'm ready to retreat into my own company.

The trip home was also a chance for some uninterrupted thinking, another benefit of having a motorcycle. I could process our conversations about stories and map out the week ahead. Yes, all this theorising about the function of stories in the commercial context was well and good but, unless I actually applied it, it wasn't worth a hill of beans. Put another way, if I wasted time talking about it instead of doing it, I wouldn't be able to afford the beans to make a hill out of.

On Tuesday I was to meet Henrik Laursen, and Charles Canterbury was to get back to me to fix up a time for our meeting. This was as it should be, if I was to have a "pipeline." Since I had met them at the Chamber of Commerce lunch I had been in contact with both, though not really on business—not at a primary level, anyway. I had spoken to the guy at the gun club, who was only too happy for Henrik to come out for a day on Lough Ree, which is part of the Shannon River system. Henrik was absolutely delighted and actually changed the date of a flight to see his family in Denmark, just so he could go out on that particular day. Apart from a bit of clay pigeon shooting on corporate days out, I hadn't held a shotgun since I was sixteen (when I'd gone out with my grandfather), but I was comfortable enough with the idea. It would be a very pleasant day out, and if you had to spend extracurricular time with a prospect, this was about as good as it was going to get.

Although that expedition was still some weeks away, I had decided to set the commercial ball in motion by setting up a meeting with Henrik's company. This was an unusual situation in many ways. Despite my ongoing, if troubled, relationship with "networking," it doesn't usually move so smoothly from canapés to a meeting in a senior director's office. My usual point of entry is via the guy who has the problem, which can be the CEO but is more likely to be a department head, who then has to get the go-ahead from his chief. So, the question was, did Henrik see himself as owner of the problem or overseer? Would my carefully crafted social relationship with him give me an inside track and improve my position?

Hard-won experience has taught me not to take anything for granted. Henrik was very senior, no doubt. Serious global companies locate significant operations of that scale in Ireland, and they put their best people at the top of them, but they don't usually put the ultimate decision-makers that far out into the field. No, indeed. Henrik could be answerable to people further up the food chain. And it's not even as simple as that. There would be an invisible web of company politics and game playing present throughout the organisation, including in its international outposts. I could see Henrik was a nice guy, but he wasn't a king, and I wasn't going to be anyone's pawn.

Early in my career, before I had a mortgage and kids (back when I could afford to take risks), I took the sales role at a rather ambitious start-up. They paid me what I'd been paid before, but the role was much bigger. The understanding was that, as I was part of the start-up and an integral element in its prospects, my stock would grow commensurate with the company's growth and achievements. We were selling big-ticket software solutions, much as I do today. Our offering was unique in a number of areas, and our mission was to go straight in and compete with the big boys. As you know, that isn't the sort of sales job that involves taking out the Yellow Pages and picking names from the page marked *P* for "prospect." After a month or so of serious homework, I had developed a list of candidate companies and accompanying leads. I identified the specific prospects within the companies and did a level of background checks that would have put a CIA agent to shame. With my jaw set, my shoulders back, and a determined look in my eye, I went at it.

After three weeks I had gotten to talk to forty people in twenty different companies. Of these, I got to meet eight. Of those, I got to second base with four. In other words, as the cops would say, I was "pursuing a definite line of enquiry." Compared to my previous sales position, this was like distilling whiskey as opposed to brewing beer. We were working with smaller quantities, but the results were richer, stronger, and more precious. Even so, I can honestly say I cannot remember which of the companies was which or who bought what. All I can remember is the big one that got away—and why.

The Irish operation was run by an expat, a very senior expat, from New Zealand named Greg. I had found my way to him through his squad—the usual line of operational people, accountants, and line managers. If he had been in the military, he would have had chevrons on his shoulder and medals on his chest. He was the cool-in-the-heat, calm-in-a-storm leader type. He listened to his lieutenants, he weighed up the information, and he appeared to be as impressed as his chiselled face would allow us to see.

Remember, we were in a start-up situation. My boss was overseeing all areas of set-up, product development, production, and shipping. All he needed was customers. So, right then, my job wasn't just to find new business, it was to find business—period. On the days that I was in the office as opposed to on the road foraging, we would pass in the corridor and he'd ask me how I was getting on. Considering the circumstances he was patient, I suppose, but I felt under pressure. I told him how far I'd gotten with Greg and he was very excited. He knew the firm, and to him, it spelled a small doorway into a big catch. And, as happens in cases of unbridled optimism, the more excited he got, the more convinced I got that a deal was going to happen.

Then came the day that Greg wanted to come and visit our facility and meet our senior personnel. Yes, we were a start-up, but we talked big, which meant that we would have to look big, too. We went into overdrive, making empty desks appear occupied and putting signage up that suggested additional offices on other floors of the building (of which we occupied only half a floor). We put flowers in reception and Danish pastries on the boardroom table. We were one stop away from calling rent-a-crowd. It seemed to work. Over a mug of black coffee at the boardroom table, Greg looked at our proposal with a decisive expression and announced:

"We need to show this to Geoff in head office."

My boss and I exchanged excited glances. I could see we both had that feeling where it seems as if your blood has been replaced with cola. A feeling of fizziness and lightness ran from my heels to my heart and then to my throat. As far as we were concerned, we were taking our proposal and contract to Greg's company's headquarters in Madrid for a ceremonial rubber-stamping. From our side of the table, this was a done deal.

We assembled the entire team that would be working on the project and booked flights and hotels for the appointed day. That was fifteen round-trip tickets from Dublin to Madrid booked at short notice, a total of thirty bed nights in a hotel carefully chosen not to look cheap in the eyes of our prospect. Our business at home was to be managed by a skeleton staff for almost three days. For a fledgling business, this trip was a big investment. It was a commitment.

Long story short, we arrived at the headquarters in central Madrid and were left waiting for half an hour before the three mandarins arrived, accompanied by Greg, who now looked less like the military leader and more like the dispatch boy. The meeting lasted forty-five minutes, which included a thorough, well-rehearsed, thirty-five-minute presentation from us, followed by five minutes of rather disinterested questioning. The tribunal then conferred amongst themselves in whispered Spanish. My heart sank into my boots. Far from the rubber-stamping exercise we had expected, it was very evident that not only were there other horses in the race, but we were far from being the leaders.

"We thank you sincerely for your presentation, which was most interesting for us. As you are being aware, we are considering other proposals for some months. We hope that we will be answering you by Wednesday of next week. Please have a safe journey back to England."

That one really hurt. They hadn't even registered where we had come from—all they knew was that we were speaking English. At no point in my meetings had Greg said anything about other proposals or about a competitive tender, but that was not his responsibility. It was my job to ask, to identify all obstacles, clear them, and if they couldn't be cleared, to call off the dogs and hunt elsewhere.

My boss's complexion was reddening from the collar up, and I knew it had nothing to do with the Spanish midday heat. I think there was a part of him that wanted to strangle me, but the reality was, he had gotten as carried away as I had. That being said, the fault was all mine. I found out everything there was to know about the company's business: what they produced, who they sold it to, what raw materials they purchased, how their export procedures worked, how many sites they had globally, the shareholder structure. You name it, I knew it, but I never stopped to ask one simple question:

Where is that decision being made?

There was nothing in the current situation with Henrik that told me this situation was any different. Henrik himself was highly qualified, but he was posted overseas. To draw a comparison, he was an ambassador, not the president. The president lives on home turf in the White House. Tuesday came around and I headed to Henrik's office, which was located within the Airport Business Centre. It is an excellent location: it's easy to reach from any part of the city or country, handy for import-export, and, for someone like Henrik, handy for trips home to Denmark.

His office, it turned out, was in the actual terminal building, with a view over the runways, which was very distracting for my inner-schoolboy. I've always been fascinated by planes. Nevertheless, I kept my eye on the ball and the meeting went as planned.

Not only had we met at the Chamber of Commerce lunch, chatting amiably, we had also spoken on the phone about duck shooting and other matters. While this gave us a level of familiarity, neither of us allowed this to affect our business conversation. My "given" from our relationship so far was that we had one another's respect, and when you think about it, that's a nice thing to know going into a meeting.

> "Thank you for inviting me in to see you, Henrik, I appreciate you're a busy man. Today, I was hoping we might focus on what it is that you want to achieve with this project. I'd like to understand what's driving it and what obstacles you've come up against or foresee. That way, I can sound somewhat intelligent when I'm answering the questions you are bound to have. If there isn't a fit between what you're looking for and what we are good at, it'll be obvious very soon.

> "Of course, if there is a good fit, then we'll probably need to talk about money and about who else you feel I should be talking to."

Henrik smiled.

"You are a man of business, I see. You are going straight to the point."

I laughed. It made me wonder if I'd been a bit brusque, so I gave him a brief version of the story I've just told you.

"Well, my philosophy is a simple one, Henrik," I said with a smile. "In business, there are three states of being: the first is downtime, when you can relax; the second is time to talk about business; and the third is doing business. When we go duck hunting, we'll be relaxing. When we met at the chamber's lunch, we were talking about business. Now, we're doing business."

"That's a very solid philosophy." He smiled and then went on to answer all three of my questions clearly and succinctly. He wanted me to talk to his technical people here in Ireland as well as in London. His organisation was not yet talking to anyone else, but a shortlist of candidate firms was being drawn up. Presumably, they would be called in for initial discussions. I was satisfied that I was in play early enough that if I considered their problem and our solution a good fit, I'd go to the proposal stage. Otherwise, duck shoot or no, I wasn't going to waste my time. It's a game of vanity, really. CEOs and their technical people like to believe they are assessing our suitability and granting us the opportunity to tender. Savvy salesmen let them believe that, but in reality, they make the decision for themselves.

I was reassured by the fact that Henrik would be part of the management panel ultimately deciding on the award. The rest of the panel would consist of two colleagues of similar seniority from other parts of the organisation. While that was nice to know, it told me nothing about when a request for a proposal would materialize or from where. I had made sure to ask for important information about the decision-making process, and I was lucky in the way I had met Henrik, which had earned me his respect. Flattering as this was, I still had to keep my feet on the ground and remember some of the RFP ground rules.

For example, just because someone has a job to be done, it doesn't mean it's a job for you. All too often, salespeople get into a feeding frenzy when they hear there is business about and don't take time to see whether it fits what they have to offer. A vast amount of time, money, and energy can be wasted, with the only return being a similar amount of disappointment. The preparation involved in responding to an RFP, not to mention the existing business that gets neglected, is considerable. An RFP is only worth responding to if the job is worth having. You owe it to yourself to cross-examine an RFP like you're an attorney at a murder trial.

Oh, it can be tempting. I know only too well. You have had a dry spell over a couple of months, with a lot of doors closing in your face. One day, someone from Acme Global Inc. calls you up with a request for a proposal. They might be a round hole to your square peg, but still you manage to convince yourself and your colleagues that this is the one that will turn things around. And you know what? In those cases, the worst thing that can happen is winning the business. At least if you lose, you can go and lick your wounds and hopefully learn the lesson to only pursue suitable business. If you win, you have the ongoing pain and discomfort of trying to service a contract that you shouldn't have in the first place. Whether it's a conflict of scale, corporate culture, and individual personalities, or an inconsistency between their pain and your solution, you'll lose money, morale will suffer, and your reputation will suffer a dent because the results will not be good.

The fact of the matter is—and this is hard for people to get their heads around—if you aren't involved in creating the RFP, then the odds are you've been included to make up the numbers. Yes, you and Sucker Inc. have been included on the list so that the board believes it's reviewing three contenders. The reality is, the winning company is the one that was there in time to formulate the RFP. To paraphrase the old military saying: It's better to be inside the tent with the flow going outward.

Are you squirming a bit? Have you been that soldier? The guy who has been drawn to an unsolicited RFP like a moth to a flame, only to get burned? If so, don't go and review the stats, because it will hurt. If you've scored more than 3 percent on unsolicited RFPs, you've done well. The only way to sidestep this is if you can identify a gap in the RFP—a weakness or an oversight that will allow you to indicate your suitability as a candidate, thereby giving you more credibility and clout. This creates a thorn in your competitor's side by highlighting a weakness in either their understanding of the problem or the suitability of their solution. Oh yes, and never make the mistake of pitching in at a lower price in the hopes of undermining the other submissions. It's a simple truth: lower your price and you'll pay the cost.

What I needed was to get Henrik to open up on his problems so that I could identify the places they were hurting. Sure, people will tell you what they see as their problems, but if you can help them discover what they haven't considered or noticed, you have given them reason to pay more attention to you. It's just like if you go to the doctor with a headache, and while you're there, he wants to take a look at a mark on your arm. You will be impressed by his thoroughness.

The flip side to this is the danger of giving too much away. If, in your desire to please and impress, you put absolutely everything you've got into your proposal, you will have nothing left for the all-important coup de grâce. Worse still, if you have been put in the tender group to make up the numbers, you are simply giving your competitor and the prospect an owner's manual for how you would have handled it. And you would be giving it to them free.

I hate to be clichéd about this, but it really is like a game of poker. You only use the cards you know are required to win the hand. You don't throw all your royal cards in just because you have them in your hand.

All of this was going through my mind as I contemplated my next step with Henrik. Things were going very well and I had every reason to believe we would be doing business together. However, without appearing rude, ungrateful, or intransigent, I had to make it plain to him that I wanted to be involved in preparing the RFP as well as responding to it.

People can be naturally coy about saying what is actually on their mind, and it helps no one. I used to think that we Irish were the worst at this, but I've since noticed it across a wide variety of cultures and countries. The typical scenario unfolds like this: You are at someone's house drinking coffee. There are biscuits on a plate, which are offered around. Everyone enjoys the biscuit, the coffee, and the conversation. Someone in the group leans forward and points at the one remaining biscuit, saying, "Does anyone want the last biscuit?"

Everyone else shakes their heads as if nothing could be further from their minds. The speaker smiles and takes the biscuit, making a wry comment about it being a long time since breakfast. Despite the fact no crime has been committed and everybody, including Mr. Second Biscuit, has behaved very well, the other people will resent his audacity. *How dare he take the last biscuit!* This is the kind of thing that separates humans from dogs, cats, and machines—all of which tend to respond in a more binary fashion. These are also the traits a salesperson has to watch for: jealousies, grudges, ambitions, and rivalries. And I don't just mean watch them as potential pitfalls—I mean watch them as opportunities for tactical storytelling.

If, for example, you realise your prospect is feeling unappreciated within their organisation, you can position your story in such a way as to make them the hero. Yes, you could say this is a cynical way of winning them over to your side, but it does help them to present themselves in a more positive light when bringing your case to a higher level. Yes, that may increase your chances, but it also helps them walk taller. This is the opposite of what most salespeople do. The usual approach is to go in as the shiny suited heroes, with stacks of case histories that show the vendor company in the heat of battle, saving the day for the client company. But think about it, who wants to be portrayed as a damsel in distress? It's much more powerful to present your past clients and customers as seriously clever people who could spot quality and talent. That way, your new prospect gets to project himself into the heroic role, as a guy who has been clever enough to arm himself with the best equipment and surround himself with the best advice.

Henrik is no giant—he comes up to about my ear—but as a man he walks tall. He led me out of the office, down a flight of stairs, and into an open-plan office area on the floor below. As he walked in the door, you could feel the atmosphere change among the twenty or so people in the room. It wasn't fear or tension. It was something more than simply respect. He was greeted with warm smiles and looks of anticipation, as if his visits to their work area were associated with good news or some sort of treat. He was both aware of this effect and used to it. He went through the room introducing me to his colleagues. Eventually we approached the corner desk, from behind which a tall man in thirties unfolded himself and stood up. Henrik introduced him.

> "Seb, I'd like you to meet Roger. Roger is head of IT, and he's the man who'll be advising me on the technical side of any proposal you may make. Believe me, he's a tough man to satisfy." He might have said this with a wink, but from the few seconds I'd been in Roger's company, I did not find it hard to believe that he would be hard to please.

I held out my hand, expecting Roger to proffer his in return. It was so slow in coming I had almost given up and withdrawn mine when he advanced his rather cold, clammy palm. We spoke generalities for a few minutes before Roger reminded Henrik of a report he had to complete before lunch. I gave Roger my card. I noticed him awkwardly fumbling, as if looking for a business card to reciprocate. I relieved the tension with a reassuring "don't worry Roger, I can never find the damn things when I want to either.

As Henrik and I left the office and headed out to the reception area, I was left with a bad feeling. Yes, it was great to have gotten in at the top level. I had Henrik's blessing, but there was a downside. From Roger's point of view, I would be seen as the stereotypically smooth salesman who had winkled his way into Henrik's good books with no real understanding of what Roger perceived as the "real" issues. By his own admission, Henrik was not an IT person; therefore, he wasn't qualified to identify me as a contender for the project. Add to that the rather hangdog persona that Roger had presented, and I knew I was in for a challenge. If I didn't play my cards right, it wouldn't matter how good anything I might propose actually was. Roger would find ways to undermine it. Listening to Henrik, however, it was obvious he had not noticed this trait in Roger. Such was the respect he commanded among his employees, he saw only the warm attitude they had towards him and not how they might appear to others.

Shaking hands with Henrik at the front door was an altogether more pleasant experience than it had been with Roger, whose hand had felt like a wet sponge. I promised to get back to Henrik with some details about the duck shoot and to communicate with Roger about the tender—in other words, to help Roger prepare the RFP. At least, that was my mission.

Back in the car, I headed out onto the motorway that skirts the city. Roger was a wake-up call. The contrast between how I felt in the initial part of the meeting with Henrik and how I felt when we were talking with Roger was unsettling. With Henrik, I had lulled myself into a false optimism: that the best proposal was going to win, that it was all about the work. But it never is. There are always the human elements. At the top, the CEO's insecurity is reassured by a big name, regardless of how slipshod their work or how much extra the name is costing. If you're from a smaller, less well-known company like I am, then he is scrutinizing you, checking for chinks in your armour, seeking excuses to scratch you off the list in favour of Big Blue. Compared to people like Roger, however, the CEO is straightforward. The guys in between, especially the technical people, have a whole other agenda. They read all the trade journals and blogs; they contribute to the chat rooms. As regards the equipment, their interest is pure. They want a system that either gives them an easy ride in the workplace or an elevated status among their tech buddies. They may believe the solution their friend developed in his bedroom is the best. What is best in their eyes may not meet the practical, end-user requirement of sales staff or other personnel. As often as not, however, it goes beyond the equipment itself. It's a sad fact of life that the majority of large, successful companies are run by people who know how to run large, successful companies. These people are rarely software developers, salespeople, laboratory boffins, mechanics, or craftspeople. They are business people, and they know how to manage money and make decisions based on a bird's eye view of their business

196

and the market in which it operates. They cannot, and do not, please all of the people all of the time. So for someone like Roger, and millions like him around the corporate world, it's frustrating for him to know that even though his work is what makes the business possible, he has little say in how the company is run. And my being in his office was a case in point. IT is his domain, yet even in IT procurement his boss sees fit to interfere and may even put his old-school-tie friends in line for the tender.

With this in mind, I spent the remainder of the journey doing a little exercise. Speculating on what Roger's issues might be, I delved deep into my mind and memory to source stories I could use to address the situation. I was looking for stories where the underdog wins; stories where the guy who isn't so tall, dark, and handsome actually gets the girl because he's cleverer; stories where brain won over brawn—or, more bluntly—stories where the back-room nerd became the boardroom hero. Again, this isn't about being dishonest, it's about showing him that I recognise his importance to the organisation and can provide him with the tools to demonstrate his qualities to others.

When I got back to my office, there were a few mails and messages to absorb and return. One of the calls was from Gordon about the next ride-out. I decided to leave this one to last, a treat to enjoy once I had been a good boy and had dealt with all the other calls. There was an email from Dominic. It was quite formal in tone; I could see it was cc'd to Alf and Karl. Nevertheless, it looked optimistic. It said they had a couple of things to straighten out and they would be back to me on Thursday. While I didn't want to read too much into it, I saw that as a good sign.

Charles Canterbury left a voicemail suggesting we meet on Friday at 12:30. He didn't say it, but this inevitably meant lunch. I'm not a big fan of the so-called business lunch. As I'd previously said to Henrik, I'm either relaxing, talking about business, or doing business. At the lunch table you find yourself pretending to relax while trying to talk about business. You achieve neither. At least we had met before and had conversations about things other than business. It was interesting that he called rather than emailed. I took that to mean he had wanted to talk about something other than just the appointment.

The remaining messages were basic housekeeping stuff. I got through them quickly enough, made a cup of coffee, and prepared to call Gordon the Shrink. I put my feet up on the windowsill and dialled his number. As I watched the city between the gap between my shoes, it occurred to me this wasn't a position I would normally sit in. I smiled as I realised I was in Harley mode. I'm not a daydreamer, but I do look forward to things. On the subject of looking forward to things, my diary was open in front of me, and the next Sunday's All Ireland Hurling Final was marked in big letters. I'd just put the dot under the exclamation when Gordon answered his direct line.

"Gordon, my friend, have you shrunk any good heads lately?"

"Two politicians, a priest, and a taxi driver. How about you? Any of those Eskimos bought your fridges yet?"

Standard locker-room banter. Neither of us really understood what the other did all day and we liked to have a bit of fun about it. I expected him to launch straight into discussing the next ride-out, but he surprised me.

"Seb," he began in a tone resembling excitement.

"You know this story thing that you and Jack keep going on about? Something occurred to me."

As I have said, Gordon has shown a healthy disrespect for the "sales function," so this had to be interesting. He went on.

"I was watching *Frasier* repeats on cable last night. It's a weakness of mine; I'm getting treatment for it. Anyway, it suddenly occurred to me that without stories, the world of psychoanalysis would be a very empty place. 'Oedipus complex'? A story. 'Napoleon complex'? Based on a story. I'm not sure everyone in my profession would agree with this as a way of describing it, but when a patient lies back on the couch in my office, I'm often talking to the pro- tagonist of a story who has reached their punchline but isn't sure what the middle, transformational part of the story was. I then try to untangle the story to see what the transformative factor—is that what you called it…?"

"Yeah, pretty much." I didn't want to interrupt him.

"I suppose what I'm trying to say," he went on, "is that you're ab- solutely right about the power of stories in human communication. Every fork in the road is a potential transition point for the sto- ries of our lives, whether it's in the sales process, medicine, sport, or education. Our work isn't that different after all!" He laughed heartily at this unlikely revelation.

"You called me to tell me that?" I said, joining in his laughter.

"No, I called to talk about the ride-out, but I thought I'd share my little insight."

He was a bit giddy. Since leaving the message with me, he had caught up with most of the other guys and there was 100-percent agreement on our destination: the Boyne Valley, an area just north of the capital filled with history, mystery, myth, and legend. It's an ideal place for anyone thinking about stories. You could say modern Irish history began in the Boyne Valley with the famous Battle of the Boyne, which took place in 1690, though it all goes way further back than that. Not far away is Tara, where the High Kings of Ireland sat at the dawn of history and told tales of Celtic superhe- roes. The area is also dotted with giant burial mounds that are actually in- tricate solar-aligned burial chambers. They predate the Pyramids by about a thousand years. It would be a relatively short trip, but it was plenty to see and an excuse for a night out.

"How many will there be?" I asked him.

"Seven," he replied. "And by the way, I presume you've heard Jack is heading home at the end of the month. This will be his last trip with us."

"Ah, no. I hadn't heard that. That's a pity; he's a good man."

It would be sad to see him go all right. Gordon and I chatted about a few more things before we hung up. I had a couple of other things to do around the office, but I got it done in plenty of time for an early trip home. There would be time for couple of sundowners with my wife before dinner.

It was a very pleasant, late summer evening as we sat back in a beam of sunlight and enjoyed a civilised drink together. The subject of conversation quickly turned to the upcoming final—hurling being a mutual passion. Hurling is a field game played between two teams using ash-wood stick and a ball – and there the similarity with hockey ends. It is both the oldest and the fastest field sport in the world, dating back about 3,000 years to Celtic Ireland. When outsiders remark that in Ireland it's seen as a game of life-or-death importance, we scoff at them and explain that it's a great deal more important than that! Every parish has its club, every county has its teams, and the championship is followed passionately as the field is eventually reduced to the two final contenders. The final takes place on the hallowed field of Croke Park in Dublin. Though tickets are gold dust, we would happily trade our mortal souls for our place in the crowd. We would attend a final regardless of which counties were playing, but the fact that our own home county was in contention made our presence there an absolute imperative.

I don't remember anything in particular about the intervening workdays. Before I knew it, my wife and our two boys were piling into the car, dressed from head to toe in black and amber like a deranged convention of Esso Tiger mascots. The first part of the journey to the city was pleasant enough, but as always, the closer we got to the ground, the more chaotic the streets became. Both groups of fans were immediately discernable by their colours, but we were all one happy family, excited by the prospect of the game.

By half-time I'd lost my voice from shouting and cheering. It was a closely fought game all the way to the final whistle—so close it ended in a draw. Frustrating on the one hand but it would prolong the season and give us a couple of weeks more excitement before the winner was finally decided at a future match. The car on the way home was a high-level summit of four expert hurling pundits analysing every second of the foregoing game.

The following week, I met up with Charles Canterbury at his city centre offices. As with Henrik, it was strange to finally meet him in his own environment and to talk specifically about work. In our previous conversations, it was as if we were avoiding the topic.

This was where Charles was at home. He knows his business inside out, from production to finance, from marketing to internal politics. I took pretty much the same approach with him as I had with Henrik—talking straight, asking what the problems were, where the pain was, and who the decision-makers were. I always remember what an old salt said to me years ago about prospecting:

> "When you're hitch-hiking, don't be blinded by the headlights. Make sure it's the right ride for you, or you really will get taken for a ride!"

Charles didn't bat an eyelid; he just answered each question as it came. He then pulled out a non-disclosure agreement.

> "We need a hard copy of the NDA, but the application can be done online. In order for you to understand what we need from you, you'll have to understand a few details about our processes. That's why we need your signature," he said, indicating the line where I was to sign.

> "The good thing from your point of view," he went on, "Is that no company wants to be handing out a whole heap of NDAs. The more we put out there, the more likely a leak and the harder to trace the leak. So that's my contribution to your success in this

tender. You are one of just three companies in the mix. From here on, it's up to you and how you impress these guys."

This was good. Of course, I still had a lot to learn about what capability gaps the tender was addressing. In other circumstances this would either be a lottery or a set-up, but here the field was limited to three participants. I was going to hold my place in this shortlisted position until I knew more. If I found it wasn't for us, I could pull out at a later stage.

He took out an A4 sheet with a list of names, titles, job specs, and contact details and handed it to me. Then—rather indiscreetly, I felt—he ran down the list using his pen as a pointer and gave me the inside track on them all, one by one. He then kicked back in his chair and put his hands behind his head.

"You got time for lunch?" he asked.

"That was supposed to have been my line!" I replied, smiling. I told him of a place nearby that I liked.

"That's great." He smiled. "I thought I'd exhausted all the possibilities in this area."

It was a Malaysian restaurant, and their prawns are to die for. Charles declined the shellfish, claiming allergy issues, and stuck with the chicken. I'm usually uncomfortable with client entertainment, and my earlier meetings had made me uneasy about this one. Perhaps it was because of my trepidation that the lunch actually turned out to be very pleasant. He talked about growing up in Alberta, going to college in Quebec, and the various postings he'd had around the world. He asked me a great deal of questions about Ireland, which showed a genuine interest beyond the superficial tourist sights. As Charles settled the lunch bill, I thanked him for both inviting me to participate in the tender and for his company at lunch. It had been a genuine pleasure, and I hoped that success in the tendering process would give us the excuse to meet up again.

202

Blinking as we walked out into the sunlight, we shook hands and went our separate ways, he back to his office and me to my car. I got in, threw my briefcase into the back, and started the engine. As I did so, the radio came on. It was the middle of the news, which, as usual, was brimming with doom and gloom. I would have switched the station, but I realised every station would have news on at this time, so I decided to sit tight and see what came on afterwards. Once the headlines were over they went on to sport, and the first item up was the rescheduled hurling final. I was impatient to hear the date they'd chosen for the rematch, and they seemed to take forever to get to the point. Eventually, the official from the sporting headquarters told us that the rematch would take place the Sunday after next. I reached for the phone and speed-dialled my wife, telling her to set the wheels in motion for tickets, assuming we'd all be going together again. I got through to her voicemail and left my message there, but rang off still feeling impatient and unsatisfied. I hate leaving messages. I'm never happy until I know my message has been received.

To take my mind off things, I tried to concentrate on other matters. I thought of Roger, his soggy handshake, and how I was going to go about winning his trust and demonstrating how much easier I could make his life. I wanted him to see I wasn't just Henrik's golf buddy. Thoughts of Henrik brought me to our upcoming duck shoot. I was thinking that it would be a good idea to make a move with Roger before the shoot so that I could run any obstacles I encountered past Henrik on the day. Mentally, I ran through my diary to work out when I could schedule a meeting with Roger, and that's when it hit me. The duck shoot was a week from Sunday, the same day as the rematch. This was a potential catastrophe.

How could I get to the match without upsetting Henrik, who had delayed his trip home to Denmark especially for the duck shoot? Missing the game was out of the question, so the first thing I had to do was to secure an extra ticket and invite Henrik. After all, these were special circumstances; no one could have predicted a drawn match, never mind the date of the rematch. It was the first match that had ended in a draw in fifty-nine years. I speed-dialled my wife again. This time I got her, and better still, I got her before she had heard the previous message. Her voice went straight into business mode and she swung into action.

Henrik's rescheduled flight was for early on Monday; his Saturday was probably still free. My two courses of action were, therefore, to take Henrik to the game and move the duck shoot to another day, which would be my preferred scenario, or to send him off on the duck shoot without me. I made a call to Derek from the gun club, who said he was OK to move the shoot but to let him know for sure by the end of the day. The last piece of the jigsaw was Henrik himself, and I wanted to wait until I was comfortably at my desk before I made that call.

Back at my desk, I took a deep breath and called Henrik's number. Business calls don't normally make me nervous, but this call wasn't just business. It was about hurling, and that's personal. I was put through to Henrik and began saying my piece.

"Henrik, I have a proposal to make to you, but first, let me tell you a quick story."

"In Ireland there's a story for everything, I am beginning to think!" He laughed.

"Indeed there is, and it's a tradition were very proud of. One of many traditions we're very proud of, like the one begun by the Irish hero Cú Chulainn and his fellow warriors more than 2,500 years ago. It's a game called hurling, where two teams of fifteen men, armed with the branches of an ash tree, compete on a grassy field.

"Back then the matches were said to continue for weeks at a time, with players dying on the field and their comrades continuing to play around their corpses. Today there are more rules and the matches are only seventy minutes long, but we take them just as seriously as our ancestors did…"

I had my story perfectly honed, and I was so proud of the way in which I was going to turn it to the point where Henrik's inclusion in our family's odyssey to the final at Croke Park was the greatest honour an Irishman could bestow upon a guest. But he stole my thunder.

"Seb, I am in Ireland long enough to know of your national obsessions. When I am hearing the news report at lunchtime today I said to myself, *Goodbye to the duck shoot.* I will forgive you this, Seb, if you can tell me one thing…" I could hear the smile in his voice as he relished the agony he was putting me through.

"And what would that be, Henrik?" I answered nervously.

"That you have a ticket for me!"

Immediately, the boot was back on my foot. When I told him that not only was he a guest of my family on the day but also that he would be duck shooting on the Saturday (if he was free), he was thrilled. The rest of the conversation consisted of details and arrangements. When I put the phone down, I paused and wondered in how many other cities that exchange could have taken place? Also, which was the more audacious, me putting a ball game ahead of a firm arrangement, or his asking me for a ticket?

It then occurred to me that it would be nice to ask Jack to join us on the hunt. Now that I knew he was leaving, I was keen to establish contact with him outside of the Harley club, with a view to keeping in touch long-term. When I called him he was uncharacteristically coy, and I think he was very flattered to be asked to the shoot.

Now I could put hunting and hurling out of my mind and concentrate on the next two issues facing me: Dominic and Roger. Dominic had left a message for me earlier on in the day, and to be honest, I had delayed responding to it. I didn't know why, but I had a bad feeling about it. I'd wanted to get my lunch with Charles out of the way first. Then, once the hurling issue had raised its head, that'd taken priority over everything else. Now it was time to face the music. Dominic had gone out on a limb for me. He was like Roger in Henrik's company; he was one of the techies who made the business hum, but his input into its management was negligible. Yes, he believed in our product, I had no doubt, but it took a lot for a guy like him to take his convictions with him up to the top floor. Now, having met Alf, my respect for and appreciation of Dominic had only increased. So, regardless of the outcome of the call I was about to make, Dominic would be appearing on my Christmas card list.

I picked up the phone and dialled his direct line.

"Hi there, Seb. I thought it would be you."

Now that was a cheerier greeting than I had expected.

"Dominic, my apologies for not getting back to you sooner. I've been out of the office. How are things with you guys?" I said confidently. By this stage I had managed to get back into a pragmatic frame of mind about it. It was either good news, bad news, or a delay. There was not room for anxiety.

It was good news. He was as excited as I should have been. That isn't to say I wasn't excited, but it hadn't fully sunk in yet. I tend to be rather matter of fact about these things until they have really sunk in, at which point I'm prone to yelling "Yessss!" at the top of my voice.

We talked for about five minutes about the whys and the wherefores. Experience had told me to ask how and when the arrangement would be finalised and how soon it would be made public. After getting those details, I put the phone down and burst into spontaneous laughter. As I laughed, something occurred to me that made me laugh all the harder. It was so simple. Dominic was my story for Roger. By adapting my experience with Dominic, exaggerating a few bits here, embellishing a few other bits there, I would have the perfect background story for Roger. Of course, I would have to be careful how I told it. I would have to make Dominic into the hard-bitten hero who had picked me as an ally in his bid to make the boardroom see reason. In fact, my role in the story would have to be virtually incidental.

Stories are about emotions. Without emotions, a story is just a series of facts with neither a heart nor a brain. For a story to work, it has to come from the heart. Aesop managed to get us to visualise a talking tortoise and a talking hare. He achieved this because the emotion he was trying to get across came from the heart. Good storytellers are able to give those stories from the heart because they have made them their own. That's why there are so many variations on the classic stories that have been passed down through the generations—each new storyteller along the way has made a change or an adaptation that gives them ownership of that tale. And so long as the four elements of setting, complication, turning point, and resolution are in there, it's still a story.

While I still had this notion running through my head, I called Roger and made an appointment to see him. With a date in his diary, I would hone back my story of the tech hero who combined his vision for the company with the valuable product of a software salesman and led his way to victory in the boardroom. Positioned correctly, I would get Roger to see Henrik's endorsement of me as a step on the path to glory rather than a devaluation of Roger's contribution.

Devious?

I don't think so. It's all a matter of perspective and perception. Right now, from Roger's perspective, the senior management don't value him highly enough and I'm an object of suspicion. All I intend to do is alter that perspective so that I am seen as an ally and the boardroom folks as ill-informed rather than inherently evil. Through this shift, Roger will realise he has my support and thus can present our case to the board with more confidence. In the meantime, I make a sale and—most importantly of all—the company makes the right decision for its shareholders.

I stopped myself short in my musings, as I caught my reflection in the window. I appeared like Blofeld, the villain in the early James Bond movies, stroking his white Persian cat while plotting the subjugation of Western civilisation.

How often we sit among friends and regale them with stories and anecdotes of things that have happened to us or events we've had told to us by others. This is something all of us do without regarding ourselves as storytellers. Indeed, as my Harley-Davidson accomplices and I have established, human beings make, live, and tell stories psychologically, anthropologically, socially, educationally, and commercially. The transition I was making now was from relating events that have *actually happened* to creating series of events that *could have happened*, so as to illustrate my point. I was mentally crossing the bridge into the territory of the storyteller—a person comfortable enough with the notion of anecdote, allegory, story, parable, and fable that I could create the story needed to achieve a particular goal.

No, I'm not aggrandising myself here. Again, it's about perspective. I am now seeing communication of ideas through the lens of functioning stories. I am no master at it, yet it's something that is working for me and is helping me see the world in a different way. Everyone from Dr. Seuss to Jesus Christ, from Buster Keaton to Warren Buffet, uses or has used stories to explain concepts and share information. When Dr. Martin Luther King Jr. drew that enormous crowd to Washington, DC, in 1963 to hear his "I have a dream" speech, they didn't come because they read the bus timetable. They didn't come because someone told them to. They didn't come because they thought they would take in a bit of sightseeing around the capital. No, they came because of the stories they had heard. Not stories of the blind being given back their sight or the dead being brought back to life, but stories of a man whose way of talking was transformational. A man who looked at the setting African Americans were in, observed the complications they faced, and saw 1963 as a turning point. The resolution was integrated education and increased protection of voting rights.

And what about my own story? What a remarkable day it had been. A succession of events, phone calls, and news that—had it appeared in an episode of a soap opera—you would laugh about, saying that it wasn't realistic for so much to occur in one afternoon. I put a call into the gun club guy to confirm the change of day for our outing and prepared to leave work.

The following week was a busy one. I had to brief my people on the Dominic and Alf deal so that we could schedule contracts, signings, and implementation. That involved a good bit of back and forth between the two companies. I had to get to grips with Charles Canterbury's issues. He had sent me information to assimilate so that I would know whether or not we wanted to proceed. Then there was my meeting with Roger. Luckily, the night before the meeting I'd gone over my planned approach—the Blofeld Approach, let's call it. I also asked myself what it was I wanted to achieve from the meeting. Sometimes a meeting is about business; other times, it's about people. For the beginning of the meeting, I decided to pull back entirely on the tender questions and instead ask Roger questions about himself and his approach. Questions are like mini-story builders because they achieve several things at once. Asking the right question enables you to show how much you know and understand a person's situation or business. It also demonstrates a certain amount of humility without making you look weak or stupid. Plus, it enables you to elicit information from the person you're talking to.

Roger was in an unusually welcoming mood. I threw in my undervalued techie story in a "you remind me of a guy I met a couple of years back" kind of a way. There were a variety of possible outcomes from telling this story, the least of which was being able to get a read on where I stood with Roger. I got more than that, not a whole lot more, but enough for me to impress upon the guy that, though the board may sign the cheques, it pays to get under the hood with the techies. Only time will tell how well I did, but I think I'm still in the running, at least.

As the days passed, the upcoming hurling match was filling more and more of my heart and brain. It's hard to explain the feeling of tribal power that wells in your stomach before a clash like that. I've followed rugby, football, and every Irish international sporting contender from boxer to snooker player, and I can honestly say there is no emotion more powerful than having your county in an All-Ireland final. It was going to be interesting to go through the experience with someone from outside Ireland standing beside me. I actually began to wonder if I would feel inhibited. Would my customary yelling and roaring be muted by the fact that I'd have a witness nearby, someone who perhaps didn't understand the emotion of it all? I put that thought behind me, knowing that if the Queen of England and the President of the United States were standing on either side of me, I would still be yelling for my team—even if I saw them put their fingers in their ears.

A WILD GOOSE CHASE

Storytelling is a game with rules and players. The player with the best story always wins.

At last, the big day came.

It's funny how, with a weekend of such manly activities, different individuals and cultures would have different notions of which was the "big event"—the hunting trip or the sporting event. For my family, however, there was absolutely no question. We were hunting one thing and one thing only—victory on the field of play.

We went in the one car, picking up Henrik along the way. There was no point in bringing any more cars into the city than was absolutely necessary. He was living in a modern apartment building on the edge of town. When he had given me the address, I'll admit I was surprised. It wasn't the sort of neighbourhood where I expected a multinational company to billet its local CEO, but when we got there, I left my perceptions at the gate. It was a condo with fully landscaped gardens, and judging by the Porsche, the Bentley, and the two BMW 7 Series in the parking lot, it probably warranted its own postcode. Henrik had seen us coming and stepped out of the front door and into the back seat in what seemed like one confident stride. I introduced him to the family, and we were off.

Often in situations when your domestic and professional worlds suddenly overlap, there's an awkwardness, as normally full and fertile minds turn into empty spaces while people search for the right thing to say. Not today. My anticipation, my family's excitement, and the nationwide throb of enthusiasm from our far-flung tribe ensured a constant drip of adrenalin. The buzz was infectious, and it was evident Henrik had caught it the moment he got into the car.

Yes, we are a tribe. A tribe defined by the geography of our roots and our passion for the game. It's a story continually on the brink of a fresh ending, rich with new twists and turns. Our story began over 3,000 years ago on the plains of County Meath, where legendary figures led teams of up to a hundred into games that sometimes lasted for days on end. The transforming moment, in the nineteenth century, was when counties began to play one another in a formal league. In that way, a country that was fighting for its independence developed a national pride in individual county units, sowing seeds of pride in the nation that was to come. That beginning will never change, nor will that turning point. But each year, as the league brings counties and teams to the final, a new ending is written. The victors will happily relive it over the twelve months ahead, and the vanquished will use it to fuel their determination to win next time.

Sporting loyalty and tradition is a worldwide experience. Just consider the baseball stadiums of the United States, the sumo wrestling rings of Japan, the rugby pitches of Fiji and New Zealand, and the ice hockey rinks of Canada. The tears that always well up in my eyes as my team marches out onto the field are as much a mark of global unity as they are of tribal affiliation.

We parked the car a good distance from the stadium. You have to be strategic about these things; it's better to have a walk you can predict than to drive further into the crowd and risk not finding a space. On top of that,

212

we always park in a carefully chosen spot that gives us an easy escape from the city once the game is over.

The sun shone in a blue sky, and though it was cold, conditions were great. As predicted, I yelled myself hoarse, almost bursting several blood vessels in the process. Occasionally, I took time to look over at Henrik to see how he was getting on in this chaotic melee of shouting, screaming, and roaring. I had nothing to worry about; he seemed positively transfixed by the whole experience, staring in open-mouthed amazement at the speed and skill of the players as they sprinted down the field balancing the ball, or sliotar, on their sticks and hitting it with breath taking accuracy while running at speeds that would embarrass Usain Bolt.

I say with great pride and joy that we won the day. This time around, the outcome of the game was never in any doubt. We got back to the car and drove a few miles away from the crowds to a restaurant we like. There we soothed our hoarse throats with a few creamy pints of Guinness and made short work of some fine steaks. We then dropped Henrik home in time for an early night, wishing him a safe and enjoyable trip home to Denmark.

As for the rest of us, we were still too full of excitement to quit such a great day. Life was good. I could safely say that, in the week gone by, I had got just about everything I could have hoped for—new business, new leads, a planned ride-out, and today—the icing on the cake—another sweet win for the greatest hurling team in the history of the sport. I think that the best part of it all was that I had more things to look forward to. Sometimes after a win there's a sense of anticlimax that follows. The elation has subsided, the adrenalin has stopped flowing, and all you can see is this long, twelve-month chasm between now and the next time you can feel this good. I'm neither a chemist nor a biologist, but I'm sure it's similar to addiction. It's at that time, on a Sunday evening after a win, that I would give almost anything to go back to the stadium—to the point five minutes before the deciding point had been scored. Strangely, when you lose a game it works differently—not that we have much experience of defeat, you understand! When the whistle blows and you've lost, your heart sinks for a moment at the thought of what could have been yours. A few hours later, however, you're returning to normal life. You haven't had such a powerful adrenalin high, so the journey back down to normality isn't so steep. This is the story with the recurring ending. The blowing of the final whistle doesn't mean "they all lived happily ever after," it means "tune in next year for the next nail-biting instalment." And twelve months is a lot of nail-biting.

This time I was immune to all that. I wasn't climbing down from the dizzying heights of the victor's podium back into the grey humdrum of a drab existence. I had a great deal of other things to look forward to in the coming weeks. We stayed up until about midnight, reliving our favourite moments of the game. I'm sure the same scenario was repeated all around the country as families and friends picked over the bones of the day's play, crowning new heroes and creating new legends. Some would have the game recorded and would be shuttling to and fro. We preferred the old-fashioned way: around the kitchen table where stories were nurtured, shaped, and polished with honour and glory rather than digital debate.

Eventually, I dragged myself up to bed. I remember putting my head on the pillow and having so many thoughts going around my head that I was convinced I wasn't going to be able to sleep, but I must have been out in about a minute. A good thing too, as I had a long four days ahead of me if I was to justify taking Friday off for the ride-out.

Things had gone so well with Roger that I was effectively writing the RFP for him, though not officially, of course. We had met once more since the tech-hero story, but we had had a couple of long phone conversations in which he'd opened up considerably. A cynic might say that my initial impression of Roger could've simply been shyness, and that he would have opened up anyway as he became more comfortable. The reality is, I had put myself several steps ahead with him by telling my story, and I'll tell you why. If I had just told him the message of that story as a series of facts or statements, I would have come over as boastful. The fact that I'd told it as a story put it in the abstract. Perhaps the most significant thing achieved by the story was the fact that I had noticed the need to tell it. On one level or another, Roger could see I had taken the time to understand his situation, his pain, his ambitions, and his ideas. Rather than just bulldozing ahead and trying to simply charm him into submission, I had demonstrated an appreciation of his place in the process.

So far, it was paying off. I had downloaded all of the necessary information from the company website and had gone through it carefully, identifying areas where our capabilities were strong, taking note of our weak spots, and building a list of questions to ask Roger. Questions are funny things. As I have said, they are your opportunity to demonstrate humility without stupidity and to show your knowledge without showing off. It doesn't matter how obvious a form, a presentation, or a demonstration is, you have to ask questions. It shows you've been listening. It shows you have a pulse. And it reassures the person you're talking with that they're not talking to the wall.

In this situation, I certainly had questions to ask. Strangely enough, my questions had little to do with the technology or the company's processes. Virtually all of my questions related to people, politics, terminology, and acronyms. Why is it every company seems to feel obliged to create its own dictionary of abbreviations?

I was up at 6:30 a.m. the next day, sitting at the breakfast table with an open notepad and planning my day. When I have a lot of things to check off a list, I have to be systematic about it, and today, I was going to have to hit the ground running. I am also careful about how I prioritize things. Obviously, some things are more urgent than others, but you have to be careful not to let courtesy fall by the wayside. I was sending a nice bottle of single malt to the guy from the shooting club to thank him for Saturday, and I wanted that to go out on the Monday with a handwritten note from me. No, it wasn't a matter of life and death, but these are the things that make impressions, and impressions make an impact. Without being mercenary about it, these things come back to you.

There was a training and orientation session in the afternoon for Dominic's team, and I wanted to be there to greet them. Again, if I didn't turn up, it wouldn't make much difference, but if I was to ensure that Dominic passed on the same sort of feedback to others that had led him to me in the first place, it was important to keep my face in the frame. Once the software was up and running and signed off on, I'd hand over all worry to operations, but in the meantime, this was still the "sales" phase.

I would spend a great deal of the morning pouring over Henrik and Roger's issues. I wondered if Henrik had said anything to Roger about the match or our plans for a duck shoot. If he had, would he care or resent it? I smiled an awkward smile to myself as I briefly imagined Roger as the Cinderella of the story, stuck toiling behind a desk while the wicked stepfather and the ugly stepbrother go off shooting duck and watching ball games.

When I spoke to him later on in the day he made no mention of it, and neither did I. He seemed in very good spirits—such good spirits, in fact, that he told me a story. It went something like this.

Before working with Henrik, Roger had been in the IT department of a state organisation—he was very diplomatic and did not disclose even which area of government was involved. The elected representatives at the department in question were under pressure to modernise their systems in line with European standards, to reduce costs, and to increase efficiencies.

So far so good.

Roger and his colleagues had been arguing for such efficiencies to be implemented for many years and were relieved to know their views had been taken on board at last. According to his description, the systems they had been using were not much more advanced than battery-operated abacuses. The weeks went by and they watched the story develop in the media, assuming that there would soon be a knock on the door from a civil-service mandarin who would ask them to prepare a tender document. Over their coffee breaks and lunches, they fantasised about what they would be looking for—comparing brand names, evaluating systems, and guessing at the possible budget allocation for such an investment.

The call never came. In fact, they gave up on the idea, assuming that the matter had drifted down the priority list—a lot of political hot air, in other words. One day, about eight months after politicians had first raised the

216

issue, the IT department had put down their abacuses, sundials, and Ouija boards to enjoy a morning coffee. Suddenly, from the other end of the table, Roger heard a cough and a splutter from behind a newspaper as one of his colleagues reacted with genuine shock to something he had read.

Clearing his throat, the semi-asphyxiated IT technician held up a newspaper, on which there was a classic photo-op picture of the politician who headed their department and the CEO of a leading multinational company, who happened to have a manufacturing plant in the city. With a trembling voice, he read the caption, which announced the successful completion of the tender process for IT equipment to bring the department in line with European standards.

To cut a long story short, Roger said, not one bit of the equipment purchased through the tender was usable. This was all because of three basic questions nobody had thought to ask because no one consulted the IT department. Six months later, another country, for which the system was compatible, was able to pick up the unused equipment at a knock-down price. It was at this point that Roger left to join forces with Henrik. To the best of his knowledge, his former colleagues are still limping along with their abacuses.

Roger's story explained a lot.

There was a call from Charles Canterbury's assistant during the morning, with an update on their RFP preparation. He said he'd been promised something by the following Monday, but not to hold my breath.

In amongst all of this, I still had to maintain my pipeline. These fish were all either hooked or nibbling the bait, but I still had to throw more hooks in.

After lunch I went into the boardroom to check on the orientation. Dominic was there with five of his colleagues, and when he beckoned me out of the room and into the corridor, my heart sank. I thought he was going to give me some bad news about the process or about how our people had implemented things. On the contrary, he was very complimentary. In retrospect, I think talking in the corridor was for the benefit of his colleagues, giving him an elevated status.

Back at my desk, I looked at my list again. It had a satisfying amount of ticks. Even at this early stage in the week, I could see a clear path through to Friday's ride-out, and before I knew it, the big day had come.

The night before I had been looking at maps of the Boyne Valley, tracing our journey from Dublin to Trim and then along the river Boyne to Drogheda and up the coast to Carlingford. I was very much looking forward to it. It was a good last ride for Jack to be going on with us. There were plenty of good sights and sites to be seen. We would have a good look at Trim Castle, the Hill of Tara, and the passage graves at Newgrange, Knowth, and Dowth. If these locations couldn't evoke good stories, I don't know what could. These are all places I had visited either on childhood holidays or on school trips. This was the first time I was visiting them as an adult without the trip being some worthy expedition that I would be questioned about later in the classroom.

On Friday morning, as I put my overnight stuff into the panniers on the back of the bike, put on my boots, and zipped up my jacket, my mind went back to the first time I'd met Jack. More precisely, I reflected on how I had felt leaving the house that day. I had spent the day before that trip planning my meeting with Dominic and Alf but I had been quite insecure and unsure about it all. I had gone out of the driveway from our house like a kid when the class bell rings, running out the door with a feeling of relief, even though the same unfinished test, essay, or equation will be waiting for him when he comes back the next day. What had happened in between? At the time, I had just taken on a new role; since then, I had grown into it. I now felt comfortable with the job and its challenges, and better still, it would continue to bring me the same level of challenge from here on. There was nothing about the sort of prospects I was targeting that would ever make my job boring or routine. I was in a business that was at the cutting edge of its sector, and whose clients would always be, by definition, at the top level.

It was a strange sensation, having these thoughts going through my mind as I retraced my steps out towards the motorway. As usual, we had arranged to meet at a service station before taking the off ramp and continuing along the lesser roads. (I was going to say minor roads, but I remembered that until about ten years before, the roads we were going to be riding on had been the main arterial routes around the country.) The service station wasn't as evocative a meeting place as the beautiful spot overlooking the valley where I'd first heard Jack's disembodied voice speak to me from the hilltop. I figured I had a couple of minutes to check the air and oil, as I was a bit early. When I stopped beside the air pump, I realised Alan, Gordon, and Jack were already there, working on some doughnuts and coffee. They hadn't seen me yet, and it was quite interesting to see what a group of middle-aged bikers looks like, standing outside a service station drinking skinny lattes and eating not-so-skinny doughnuts. I decided to join in this classic "husbands-on-the-loose" behaviour by investing in a few doughnuts and a litre of milk for myself, feeling a sense of utter rebelliousness about drinking from the carton.

There was a festive feel to the gathering. It had been a while since we were out on the road, and there was a lot catching up to be done, with stories of summer holidays, sporting achievements, and anecdotes about kids, all underpinned by bike talk: Dyna versus Softail, Sportster versus V-Rod, Fatboy versus Road King…the unique dialect of a semi-secret society that enables members to talk with one another the world over but sounds like double Dutch to anyone outside the group.

Jack sought me out and came over to say hello in his own inimitable way.

"Taking us back into history on this trip, eh, Seb?" he asked.

"You could say that. First stop is only just over 800 years; the furthest we go back is 5,000—before the Pyramids."

"You can learn from a lot of mistakes in 5,000 years. A lot of stories to be told." He almost snarled.

"If walls could talk…" I replied off-handedly.

"They might," he replied. "I'm sure they'd have some fascinating stories."

I asked him if he'd been out this way before, and he said he hadn't but he had read up a bit about it. From my encounters with Jack in the past, I took this to mean he was probably an expert on it all. Brian and Alan came over and joined us, and we continued talking about the places we were going to visit and what we might see.

"Trim Castle is the one they used in the movie *Braveheart*," offered Alan.

"Wasn't that about Scotland? Why didn't they shoot it there?" asked Brian.

"A good question," I said. "But I'm not complaining. They must have spent a fortune in Ireland while they were filming. But there must be plenty of castles left in Scotland?"

"I came across two reasons for shooting most of it in Ireland," said Jack. "One was the tax breaks given to people making movies in Ireland. The other was that the Irish military let its men be used in the battle scenes."

There was general laughter at this.

"Do you know how many people there are in the Irish army, Jack?" Alan said with a smile.

"Yup," he answered. "Eighty-five hundred, when you count all services. You could make a pretty good battle scene with that, I'd imagine."

We were a bit taken aback, partly by Jack's knowledge but mainly because we were guilty of exposing Ireland's inferiority complex. Even though one of my heroes, Eoin Larkin on the Kilkenny hurling team, is in the army, I still had no idea Ireland's defence forces were that large. While I was processing my ignorance, Jack had more.

"As I understand it, it was a question of money and cooperation. You have to pay extras on a movie set. If you get an army in as extras, you pay for an army of extras. Then someone pointed out that the army were being paid anyway, and a day standing out in the cold wearing costumes, obeying orders barked at them by Mel Gibson, was as good as the training they were going to get on an ordinary day. Presto! Ireland gets the lion's share of a Hollywood budget."

"That's a bit of private-sector opportunism from a government-department," said Alan. "If we could have a bit more of that going on, we'd see a lot more action in return for our taxes."

There was general muttering and chatter. Then, just as a flock of starlings—or a "murmuration," as I believe it's called—changes direction without any evident signal, we eight men gravitated towards our motorcycles, donned our helmets and gloves, and straddled our saddles. I looked around the service area to make sure the way was clear before heading out onto the motorway, and yes, as always, there were children's faces pressed against car windows and fathers and husbands looking forlornly in our direction. We were off.

Technically speaking, the motorway, autostrada, freeway, or autoroute is the enemy. It's a bland, featureless strip of liquorice across the countryside, and the biggest challenge for a motorist—on two wheels or four—is staying awake. I left out autobahn because I'm told the German autobahn has no speed limit, which must make life a little more interesting. Today, as I merged with the Friday traffic, picking up speed as I overtook the commercial vans and people carriers, the motorway was my runway, and I was taking off for a blue-sky weekend.

From Trim Castle we would head to the Hill of Tara, seat of the High Kings of Ireland. We would overnight in the village of Kells. The next day we would head down to Slane, site of several historic rock concerts, our real destination being Newgrange. There was also talk of visiting Ireland's most divisive battlefield—the "ground zero" of modern Irish history—the site of the Battle of the Boyne. After that we would head north to Carlingford for the night, where I intended to eat a lot of shellfish (for which the bay is famous).

I have to be careful at home to "grease up" these trips—to make them dirty, macho, and full of punctures, engine failures, and cold billets. If I was careless and made our ride-outs seem interesting and comfortable, I'd be forced to leave the Harley behind and bring the family in the car. And it has to be said—this was a premium-quality weekend. It had all the stimulus and interesting stuff you would get on a guided tour but with the freedom of doing it your own way.

When I saw the first signpost for the off ramp, I slowed down and checked my mirrors to make sure I had the others in view. Ideally on a Harley ride-out you move in a staggered, zigzag formation so you're not quite as wide as two abreast and you can close in to a single file easily if it becomes necessary. I'm afraid I'm not always that well behaved. This was my part of the world; I knew where we were going so I was being a bit freestyle. If I didn't take care and keep a look out, somebody was going to end up in Sligo—a nice part of the world, but it wasn't where were headed. All was well. In a glance I could see Gordon, who had obviously had the same idea and was slowing down before the ramp. By the time the turn-off came, we were all in a line like a motorcade, peeling off the motorway and onto the road for Trim. It was a beautiful day. The air was crisp with a slight chill but the sky was bright blue, which always puts me into a good mood. We carried on at a comfortable speed, and everyone stayed together with nobody doing any heroics.

We reached the town of Trim soon enough, and the first thought that crossed my mind was how similar the view I was getting from my motorcycle must have been to the view horsemen riding across the plains must have got when they approached the castle centuries ago. It was easy enough to mentally blank out the telephone wires and satellite dishes. After that, it was easy enough to imagine William "Braveheart" Wallace and Edward Longshanks duking it out over the battlements. Or, to be more precise, the Norman invaders and the Gaels, whose struggle was Ireland's equivalent of the one Braveheart fought against the Anglo-Norman's in Scotland.

We pulled up in the car park and dismounted.

"Do you know what gets me?" Jack began. "The people who built places like this had no concept of DNA, and they had a life expectancy of less than fifty years, yet they were prepared to spend decades building castles that they might not live to see completed. See, it says here "the initial castle, built in 1172, was attacked and burned down a year later. Edward de Lacy immediately rebuilt it."

"I don't think you rebuild something like this immediately!" Brian said with a laugh.

"My point exactly," Jack went on. "He began the rebuild in 1173 and died before it was finished. His son finished it in 1224—fifty-one years it took to rebuild. And, like I was telling you, that was a lifetime."

We began looking for evidence of the 1995 *Braveheart* shoot and found nothing, apart from the sign saying it had happened. It's interesting to see how some things are more permanent than others. The walls had been standing for most of a millennium and would be there for some time yet, but our footprints, our bikes, and even our bones would be gone in less than that. I got rid of the morbid image in my mind. Jack was just ahead of me, drinking it all in. He was reading any signage he found, but mainly he was surveying the stonework, studying the masonry and archways. I sensed that because of the research he had already done, he was merely reading the signage to be sure they'd got it right!

"Hey Jack, I sense a whole lot of useful stories to be gleaned from this place."

"It's like I said to you early on: walls can tell stories. Look at these closely enough and you can probably tell which guy placed which block and when they took their lunch breaks."

"The biggest story this is telling me is how, if you build something right, it's going to stand the test of time and it's going to last," I said, my eyes wandering up the wall to the sky above, where a few crows where criss-crossing, adding to the atmosphere.

"But it didn't last," said Jack, surprising me.

"What do you mean?" I replied. "We're here, standing beside walls that have stood for a millennium. How can you say it didn't last?"

"Yeah, but the real trick would be if the castle was still in use," he went on. "With a roof across the top and the descendents of the de Lacy guy who started building it still in it. The transformative element in the story of this castle is the bit that brought it down."

I didn't really get where he was going. It was as if he was being argumentative or contrary—just for the sake of it.

"But castles aren't really relevant anymore..." I began, a bit feebly.

"You tell that to the folks at Bunratty, the Tower of London, Edinburgh, Quebec, or Windsor. There are plenty of castles being used today. The ones that aren't in use, like this, were either beaten by the competition or they failed to adapt and survive."

He saw the puzzled and slightly frustrated look on my face and smiled.

"Don't get me wrong, Seb. None of this actually matters. This building fascinates me, sure, but I don't give a diddly-squat whether it sits here as a ruin or whether it's the seat of government. For me it's an illustration of the human condition."

He was in a pensive mood, and I didn't have an answer. Mind you, he hadn't asked a question. We ambled along, drinking in the scale of the place and listening out for any stories the walls might have to tell us.

"This wasn't a home," Jack said absently. "It was a place of business—its business being protecting and producing on the lands around it. And in the world of business there's no 'intelligent design'; no, sir, it's all survival of the fittest. This building, and the folks that built it, somehow outgrew their relevance. Whether you are an individual, a dynasty, or a business, you are only as big as your last success. And if someone else comes along with a bigger success, you are out on your ass and out to grass."

I started laughing.

"Jack, I don't know what's got into you, man, but you're in one dark humour. Is the prospect of leaving Ireland getting you down?"

"I'm sorry, buddy. These places just make me think."

I patted him on the shoulder.

"Well, I have good news for you and bad. The next place we're visiting doesn't even have walls, but on the plus side, to us Irish it's pretty much the home of the story. And when you think of how full of blarney we are, that makes it a pretty auspicious national monument."

He seemed to relax as we walked back out into the sunlight. We had walked out of the central keep of the castle and were now walking across the surrounding park—for want of a better word—inside what they call the "apron" wall.

"Yeah, I'm looking forward to Tara. Quite excited about that."

"Not excited the way you were about this place, I hope!" I said, ducking his punch as he made to thump me on the shoulder. We joined the others at the front of the castle.

"Well, gentlemen," said Gordon. "Shall we get moving?"

"It's the reason we're wearing these strange suits!" said Brian, and we were away.

Everyone was starting to loosen up. As eight guys who spend most of their time working at day jobs, doing stuff around the house, or being there for their kids, it always takes us a while to come to terms with the fact that this time, it's about us. That this Friday we aren't at work, we are not on a family holiday, and we don't have to worry about replacing the washer on the outside tap, rust priming the front gate, or being a taxicab for our children. Our wives would not agree with this evaluation, but if you were here to see the transition, you would. Our gatherings at the meeting point, a service station or wherever it might be, is like a midmorning coffee break. Or put another way, they are like the gatherings that occur just prior to a seminar or workshop. People are talking and laughing, but it's almost as if they still have one eye on their watches. By the next stop, there is a subtle but perceptible sense of "playing truant." You'll see guys checking emails on their phones and calling their voicemails—even when they haven't received alerts. Others will call the office for no particular reason. I've learned to read the facial expression of someone who suddenly finds they've made an entirely unnecessary call and now have to come up with a justification. I imagine that the person at the other end of the line, who likely has everything under control, doesn't need the person they're covering for taking up any of their valuable time. In this regard Brian and Antonio were the most relaxed. Being a dancer and a chef, respectively, the diurnal rhythms of the deskbound nine-to-fiver are alien to them. Fleetingly, I wondered if this was a factor in Jack's rather morbid humour, but I quickly dismissed the thought. Odd he may be, but I did not see Jack being weighed down by such conventional routines and reflexes.

I don't pretend, for one second, to be immune to these factors myself. As I opened up the throttle and headed out onto what was once a national route but was now a quaint country road, I felt the stresses melt away.

I am the luckiest man or husband alive. I count my blessings routinely, but one of the reasons my marriage is successful is that my wife and I recognise and respect how different we are. I have seen so many relationships trip, stumble, and fall because spouses kidded themselves that they could read one another's minds, finish one another's sentences, and order one another's meals. If that's working for you, I'm happy for you. More than that, however, I hope it *keeps* happening for you, because the day you misread her mind, she puts the wrong end on one of your sentences, or you order the wrong meal—things will change.

I sometimes joke that if I had wanted someone who thought the same way as I did, I would have married a man, but that would never work because he'd probably look like me. Anyway, the flip side—I won't say downside— to recognising that we are different in fundamental ways is the assumptions we make.

"She is a woman; therefore, she..." or "He is a man, so he will..." Believe me, that can be just as dangerous.

I look back over the last month, and between working long hours, fixing stuff around the house, helping the kids with their study, visiting parents, going shopping, and all the other routine stuff, I have not had one half hour to devote to something that is specifically mine.

"Don't you read in bed?" I hear you say. By the time I get to bed, I'm lucky to remain awake five minutes before I crash and burn.

"But what about that motorcycle of yours?" you say.

You may remember I checked the tyres at the meetup. I hadn't had time to do that in the previous weeks, and as for changing the oil, don't ask. I can safely put money on any of the other married guys in the group having exactly the same experience. But if you were to ask our wives, I can guarantee they would think we hadn't a care in the world and that we had left them, along with all our other worries, behind us in a trail of Harley exhaust. And I don't begrudge them that perception, because I know we make reciprocal assumptions.

It occurred to me, as the landscape whizzed past, that perceptions like this are hard to shift, but it would probably be most effectively done through stories. The remainder of that leg of the journey I spent trying to construct suitable stories for sorting out the whole Mars-Venus face-off, with some hilarious but unprintable results.

My reflexes and actions all judiciously followed the rules of the road and my concentration was full, but the thinking part of my brain was off in another world. As a result, I found myself riding ahead of the others. I was the first to pull into the car park at the Hill of Tara. Rather than wait for the others, I dismounted, locked my helmet to the bike, and went walking. It's a phenomenal place—everything and nothing all at once—a bit of bumpy farmland on the one hand, a sacred site on the other. I went in and sat on a slope of grass to ponder as I waited for the others to arrive.

How do I explain Tara?

If you look at satellite images, it looks like a bad cartoon of an alien. There's an oblong head, a narrow neck, and two rather spiral eyes close together. Yet all of it is grassy field. The shapes in the landscape are the last remaining imprint of what was a complex of buildings and enclosures, which were of enormous importance for thousands of years. There's a passage grave here that's dated 3,400 BC, and the site remained in continuous usage until the Norman invasion of Richard de Clare in 1169.

Over the grassy mound in front of me, a troupe of leather-clad figures appeared. Even at this distance, I could tell that Jack, Alan, and Brian were in deep discussion. I stood up and ambled towards them, reaching them in time to hear Alan say:

"So, Jack, you want stories? This is the well from which Ireland draws its stories—mythical, political, social, and spiritual."

"This was where the Irish High Kings ruled, right?"

"You'll hear and read many versions of this story, Jack, but I'm sticking with the one I like. Back in the day there were loads of chieftains, or kings, in Ireland, each owing allegiance to another. The four most powerful, as I understand it, were the High Kings— one for each of the four provinces. The version I like is that Tara was their Switzerland or Norway—the neutral territory where they would go to iron out their differences in an atmosphere of trust. One of them would be chosen as the King of Tara, but, by definition, this was a symbolic title as the place was neutral territory."

This wasn't how the teachers had told it to me in school, but there are as many stories about what Tara actually was as there are about what went on there. I have to say I liked Alan's version, and evidently he wasn't the only one to have heard it that way.

"The version I heard said that the kings would meet there once a year during one of the Celtic feasts—Bealtaine or Samhain—a day with astronomical significance," Brian said. "And because they may have been at war or had grievances with one another outside of Tara, they had to show their commitment to the process. On arriving at Tara, each king would take off his ring—his seal or signet, I suppose—and place it in a bowl at the entrance of Tara with those of his rivals. They would then gather in the hall where they would drink—probably mead or cider—from a 'mether,' or friendship cup. This was a mug that was square instead of round. Thus, it had four handles and four lips, one for each of the four High Kings, who, by drinking from the same vessel, could demonstrate their ability to live together harmoniously."

Jack couldn't contain himself. "This is good shit!" he said without ambiguity.

Alan agreed.

"I hadn't heard that part of it, but it ties in nicely. And Jack, the reason I'm drawing your attention to this is the question of whether or not it's true."

Jack looked puzzled. "Well, is it?" he muttered.

"That's the point," Alan said, in a tone of fake exasperation. "It doesn't matter whether it's true or not. It's a good idea and it fits together nicely in a story. Isn't that the whole thing about stories? It's not that they *are* true, it's that they *could* be true, and the world would be a better place if we could learn from that possibility."

He was right. It was funny to see this notion of stories taking hold amongst the group; like sparks among the stubble, it was catching fire. Jack had come back to life since our discussion beneath the walls of Trim Castle.

"Whether they happened or not is immaterial," he said. "These stories are designed to sell an idea. By selling the idea of cooperation between the chiefs, people believed that harmony existed and therefore supported it. I tell you, there are very few stories out there that aren't selling something—whether it's an idea, an ideology, or something physical. Even history isn't immune to this. History only gets recorded, remembered, or recalled if it can be used to prove something."

Jack was in full flight, but Brian interjected.

"Is it always about selling, Jack?"

"Well, when I say selling, I guess I mean influencing as well as transacting. I agree it might be stretching a point to describe preachers or politicians as salesmen, but in many ways they are selling a message because they are trying to persuade you to believe

230

something and then to act upon those beliefs. How different is that from trying to persuade someone to like your car and then buy it?

"There's buying and there's selling. You can come into my store with a predetermined idea of what you want and purchase it. That's buying, and I—the salesman—have had nothing to do with it. As soon as I say, 'I have some hard to get accessories in stock if you'd like to see them?,' then the situation has gone from you buying to me selling. And as soon as I start selling, I'm going to be asking questions and I'm going to be giving you anecdotes. Rational left-brain information and emotional right-brain information. And whether you're a preacher, a politician, or a salesman, a story is the Trojan Horse that get's you into the emotional right-brain long enough for the core idea to leak into your rational mind."

Brian shook his head.

"Darn. I'll buy that—you had me at 'Once upon a time!'"

Jack laughed in a shy kind of way, as if he felt he might have gone overboard. Self-consciously, he went on.

"So what other stories have you drawn from this rich well of yours, eh? Has it been visited by gods? If you stare at the horizon long enough, do you see dead people?"

Cormac, who had been uncharacteristically quiet up to this point, chimed in.

"Well now, it's funny you should say that. I can't say whether they're true or not, being an atheist myself, but I've heard four stories about this place that would fit into that line of thinking. One is that it's the dwelling place of the gods. Another is that it's the entrance to the next world. One bunch claims it's the capital of the lost city of Atlantis. And this last one you are not going to believe: about a hundred years ago, a fundamentalist sect came here with shovels and began digging; they were looking for the lost Ark of the Covenant—you know, the box that contains the original Ten Commandments!"

There was a muttering of disbelief, which turned into unrestrained laughter. Then Brian asked:

"Tell us, Cormac, did Indiana Jones arrive in time to stop them?"

When the laughter subsided, Alan went on.

"It is said that one hundred and forty-two kings were crowned and reined here. Let's put that in perspective: England has had approximately seventy-two monarchs."

It was my turn to chip in.

"And do you know how the kings were chosen?" I turned to face the other direction, and they all swivelled around with me.

"At the far end of that level patch, there were two sacred stones standing side by side, not far apart. Candidates for the throne had to ride their chariots at full tilt towards the stones. When the right challenger approached, the gods would cause the two stones to move far enough apart enough for the chosen one to pass through."

Jack obviously liked that one. His face lit up like a Cheshire cat.

"That is beautiful. On the one hand, it's like King Arthur removing the sword from the stone—all full of sacred Merlin-magic. But in reality, it's just a game of prehistoric 'chicken.' Who do you want to lead you? The guy who doubts himself? The guy who gives up? Or the guy who gives it his all? Are the stones still there?" Jack's eyes scanned the field as we chorused a negative.

Jack didn't miss a beat.

"I'd bet if they were, they'd be about two inches wider than the average chariot. In other words, wide enough for Ben-Hur to get through but not for a lesser charioteer. It was a simple skill and confidence test, but those kings and their subjects bought into it because of a good story. And the result? The other three guys accepted him as the winner, and peace covered the land until it was time to test another king's mettle."

There was a lot of nodding and the sound of metaphorical pennies dropping. Jack was on form.

"Had you heard the one about St. Patrick?" asked Max, making it sound like he was about to tell a joke. When we indicated that we had not, he went on.

"They say St. Patrick turned up here to try to turn them away from the pagan gods and to take up Christianity. It's an interesting story because we know St. Patrick was a historic figure who lived in the fifth century, a good six hundred years before the Normans."

"That's an interesting one, Max," I said. "Do we know if he had any luck? Because that sounds like a good basis for the story of St. Patrick banishing the snakes from Ireland—like he was casting out demons or expelling the pagan gods."

Max laughed, shrugged his shoulders, and gestured to the land around us with his palms upward.

"The evidence is here," he said. "The period during which pagan activity began winding down here coincides with the rise of Christianity. So that's your story. Either by conversion or conquest, St. Patrick's influence overturned the pagan ways. Then, by turning it into a story about banishing snakes, they assured that every peasant farmer or hunter-gatherer in the land would toe the line to avoid being turned into a toadstool by this new wizard and his gods."

There was a lot of nodding at the plausibility of this. I kept my mouth shut about the storytelling aspect of it because, if that was how the St. Patrick banishing snakes had come about, it was using stories for lies and manipulation. I didn't want anyone accusing me of that; salesmen get a hard enough time already.

There was no doubt about it. Tara had captured our imaginations. We hadn't actually moved more than ten feet from the point I'd been sitting on the mound. It didn't matter, because we could see it all from that spot, and we'd had our fill of the atmosphere. We panned our eyes across the undulating grass, where the mounds and ridges gave Tara the look of a badly lain carpet. The gentle bumps were smooth and virtually interrupted.

"What's that over there?" Jack pointed a bit of a way across the field to a white, phallic-looking stone standing proud above the field. We walked towards it, each sharing our theories about it. Again, Alan appeared to be the most authoritative.

"That's the Stone of Destiny. The Stone of Destiny, or 'Lia Fáil,' was the stone on which the kings would stand for their coronation. It is said that when the rightful king stood on it—presumably the guy who'd ridden his chariot between the other two stones—the stone roared with joy."

With quite a serious expression, Cormac took up the story as he understood it.

"And whether we believe that part of it or not, this stone, or the one it replicates, is where modern Irish history starts to emerge from the mists. One of the reasons the stone isn't here, we are told, is that in 500 AD the High King Murtagh mac Erc loaned it to the King of Scotland for his coronation. It never came back. Later, when the English conquered Scotland, they took it; since then, English monarchs have been crowned on what they call the Stone of Scone. Oh yeah, and in 1996 they leant it back to the Scots, but they want it back for their next coronation!"

234

This prompted a lot of chatter made up of respectful awe for the stone's history and of ridicule at the idea that a piece of rock could be such a totem. Cormac went on.

> "Is it true? As Alan said earlier, does it matter? The elements within the story add up to an explanation for how things came to be the way they are, and isn't that what stories do?"

He looked at me and Jack, pausing before he went on.

> "What we can verify, historically, is that there was a battle here during the 1798 rebellion against English rule. Four hundred rebels were killed and buried on this spot. Think about it. For a people fighting for independence, what more sacred ground could those men be buried on? And what more potent symbol to mark the grave than the Stone of Destiny?"

This time there was a hushed silence as we all realised we were standing not on a 5,000-year-old tomb as we had thought but on a 200-year-old grave.

It had been an intense forty minutes, that was for sure, and such a contrast to the way we had reacted to Trim Castle just two hours before. I wondered was this symptomatic of our transition from working stiffs to men of leisure. Had we relaxed to the point where we could now get completely absorbed in our immediate surroundings without contamination from the rest of our lives?

I unlocked my helmet from the bike, but before putting it on, I stared back across the mounds that made their vague statement in the grass. I lined the image up in my mind and set it against the solid, tangible reality of Trim Castle, deciding that it wasn't the distance from our routines that had allowed us to be so engaged by the Hill of Tara, it was our imaginations. There is no doubt about it—Trim Castle is a fantastic place whose history is full of excitement, drama, and humanity. But it is documented history, information formally recorded and shared by teachers and historians. Tara, on the other hand, is built on stories and built of stories. Do we have more to learn from the notion that a man can chase a perceived evil out of a country, as if he were herding snakes, than we do from the more prosaic names and dates of a historically recorded invasion?

I'm not even going to attempt an answer to that. It is simply the watershed between "histories" and "stories"; between things that are "fact" and things that are "true." None of these things are mutually exclusive, of course, but I believe a story can change your heart where a history can only change your mind.

Back on the bikes, we headed north towards Kells, where we were to spend the night. It was still a beautiful day; the sun had moved over towards the west and the shadows were getting longer. I found the bed and breakfast I had booked, had a shower, and headed towards the bar at which we had arranged to meet. Jack walked in the door about five minutes after me, and I wished I had laid a bet with the barman on what he was going to say.

"What in the Sam Hill is a lighthouse doing here? We're darn near thirty miles from the sea."

It is a surreal feature known as the Tower of Lloyd. An eccentric built it in the 1790s as a monument to his father, and it was used as a viewing point for hunting and horse racing. The whys and the wherefores of this anecdote brought us easily back in to the subject of stories and their application.

Since I had first begun talking with Jack on the subject of stories as a business tool, I had gone from being an innocent, to being a doubter, to being a convert. Now it was second nature for me to make an argument, express a message, or deliver information through stories. Talking with Jack on the subject now, I felt much less like a disciple or pupil and more like a peer. During our first few conversations I had felt like "Grasshopper" to his "Master."

Jack has an incredible memory for other people's information. He cross-examined me about virtually every lead, client, pitch, and tender I had mentioned during our foregoing conversations. I was a bit embarrassed by this as I felt I knew little, or could ask little, about his business. At this point in life in general, and in my relationship with Jack in particular, I felt comfortable enough asking him:

"How do you remember so much of other people's information? I've heard you talking to other people too. You remember everything we've told you!"

He laughed a long laugh, shaking his head as he answered.

"Seb, you're not going to like it. I'm basically a one-trick pony!"

"What do you mean? I asked.

"Well, look at it this way. When I want someone to remember something I'm telling them, I try to make it into a story so they'll remember it. In the same way, when you tell me something, I remember it as a story. No offence to your business, Seb, but it makes it more interesting too!"

He laughed again, but I could see a cautious look, as if he was worried he had insulted me. When he seemed satisfied that he hadn't, he went on.

"It's all just about how you store stuff in your head. I think I've said to you before, I see the mind as a library. When new stuff comes in, you have to file it so you can find it when you need it."

The line between where life ended and stories began had now blurred itself out of existence. When we looked at stories in their four steps of status quo, challenge, transformation, permanent change, they covered everything.

"Jack," I said. "I'm beginning to think there are just two types of information humans can store or exchange: stories or chaos."

He nodded, pausing to gather his thoughts before continuing.

"We're social animals, which means that we have communication as well as instinct—it's a killer combination. Tell me, Seb, what are the two most formidable predators of the oceans?"

"Pardon the pun, Jack," I replied, "but that came out of the blue!

Let me see. The great white and the killer whale?"

"Great white and orca," he said approvingly. "And the difference? The great white is purely instinctive, no social. The great white does not tell stories. From the day it's born to the day it dies, it follows its instincts. If it lives, it passes on whatever worked well to its progeny. If it dies, its failures go with it. After a hundred million years, it's done quite well. But, based on what you said, the shark's life is based on chaos.

"Now the orca's life, on the other hand, is based on stories. Whales only entered the sea less than fifty million years ago, so orca's are pretty young—but they are social. They tell each other stuff. Whether it's verbal, through squeaks and squawks, or visual, through acting out, I don't know. Scientists have actually observed one orca making a discovery, sharing the discovery, and that new discovery being adopted by the group. The most spectacular example I saw was of four orca's lining up, side by side, and charging at an iceberg to dislodge a seal, which they then shared amongst themselves."

"So the whales actually got in a huddle and said, 'Listen, guys, here's how it's going to go down'—then they acted like a line of forwards in a football game?"

What this had to do with sales wasn't immediately clear, but I'm a Discovery Channel addict so I was lapping it up.

"That's exactly it. And what I try to get through to people is that they can be sharks as salesmen. God knows we've all met them—sharp suits, sharp manner, and sharp teeth. They make sales but they don't make relationships, which means that every time they go to market they have to start afresh."

He smiled as he saw it dawning on me. All this David Attenborough stuff was gradually slipping into place.

"Or, they can be orcas as salesmen. They'll get results, they'll make sales, but they'll do so by working with people. They'll do this by influencing people's thinking and behaviour and by sharing their good fortune, their advice, and their product. I'm sure there are other ways of doing it, but telling stories sure works. It wins hearts, it wins minds, and it wins business. The stories help you make the sale, but like I say, stories can also help you remember stuff about people that will win you business. And the incredible thing about it is that it actually takes less effort. You do it right and not only will the sale come more easily, the sale will go out there and bring back your next sale for you."

I understood everything he'd said. It actually helped me bed down everything I'd learned over the previous months. I was about to ask him if he could remember the name of the show he'd seen about the orcas when the door opened and the others came in. Predictably, conversation went back to the lighthouse.

What else is there to report? Is this a story that ends with a "happily ever after" permanent change following Jack's transformative presence, or is it more like the hurling match—to be continued next year? I guess it's a mixture of both.

The way I see it, life is like a sports league: There are games, there are seasons, there are leagues, and there are titles. You can excel, you can pull a hamstring, you can get the red card, and you can retire. And with every one of these steps, there's a "to be continued." Meeting Jack and getting a new perspective on how we interact with colleagues, customers, and clients has helped me up my game and graduate to a different league.

The next day we rode on to Slane, where several amongst us looked out over the natural, grassy amphitheatre by the River Boyne where famous rock concerts have taken place. Each one of us inadvertently declared our age by announcing which ones we had attended. From there we went on to Newgrange, which is incredibly impressive and prompted a great deal of discussion, but for me it was still the stories of Tara that took root in my psyche.

We had the predictable country pub carvery lunch presented by an important-looking man in a floppy chef's hat and blue gingham trousers. After that we went to the site of the Battle of the Boyne, where two claimants for the English throne had had a turf war in the 1690s, taking the turf out from under the peasants' feet and leaving them to squabble over whose religion was better than whose. When I'd heard that the site was being opened up as a tourist attraction, my first reaction was that someone had gone crazy. Now that I've been there I think everyone should go and be reminded of how crazy wars are and how little they solve. It was a fascinating place, but perhaps not the ideal choice for our last stop of the day. It seems strange to say that I was "quiet" on the bike, as I had no one to talk to anyway, but there's no other way to describe the way I felt.

We had a long coastal run from Drogheda up to Carlingford, where we checked in to our hotel, performed ritual ablutions, left our leathers behind, and re-emerged in civilian clothing. Having been in the town before, I had been sure to book us into the restaurant I wanted. By 9:30 p.m. you weren't going to be able to see me behind the pile of mussel, scallop, cockle, clam, crab, and lobster shells.

Getting back into his seat after a trip to the bar, Jack pointed at a picture of a bird on the wall.

"Hey, you get those here? I've seen something like that up in Canada."

"Let me tell you a story about that one, Jack," I said with a wry smile. "That's a barnacle goose. It spends the summer in Ontario,

Yukon, Northern Territories, and Alaska, and then it flies here for our famous mild winters.

"Now I'm sure you know that for centuries the good Catholic folk of Ireland were not allowed to eat meat on Fridays and had to stick to fish?"

"I did not know that, no." He was paying firm attention.

"Well," I continued. "The clever monks, who were a bit tired of fish, had also worked out that nobody had ever seen the eggs of that bird. All people knew was that it came in from over the sea. And do remember, that was at a time when Ireland was the edge of the world and America wasn't even a twinkle in St. Brendan the Navigator's eye.

"Finding some odd-looking shell on the beach that was otherwise unaccounted for, they made up a story that these were the eggs of the bird in question. And as the eggs were found at sea, they weren't birds at all—they were fish. Presto, the monks were able to enjoy goose meat on Fridays right into the 1960s, when fish was no longer a requirement. The shells the monks had found were actually a type of barnacle, now known as the 'goose barnacle,' reciprocating the name 'barnacle goose.'

"Now, Jack," I smiled. "That's what I call good use of stories!"

EPILOGUE

When you have your ducks in a row, you can shoot for the stars.

Driving westward in the morning light, we were racing with the shadows as the sun, emerging over the horizon behind us, created long treelike silhouettes on the landscape, pointing us towards our destination.

Dawn has to be the most beautiful part of the day, though I can't say it's a period I'm over familiar with. In spring and summer dawn occurs before I get up, while during winter I'm either at my desk or behind the wheel of a car, neither of which is an especially suitable vantage point from which to contemplate the birth of a day. It was only on rare occasions like these that I could actually drink in the extraordinary atmosphere. Everything around us was fresh with dew that glistened and sparkled in the sunlight. Cattle looked up, nonchalantly scolding us with their eyes, as if telling us we'd already missed the best of the day. Birds rushed about with all the busyness and frenzy of their human counterparts in the city we had left behind.

We had been on the road since about 5:30 a.m. We met Derek at the gun club for a bit of a crash course with the guns before heading out to the marshes. As I listened to him instruct us on safety, loading, aiming, firing, and then safety again, it all seemed very simple. It occurred to me how important it must be, whether in a war zone or on a duck hunt, for a gun to be simple to use. If you want to out-manoeuvre the finely honed reflexes of a wild duck, you have to be able to move fast. It gave me a rather strange feeling to be holding a gun. The engineering and craftsmanship felt exquisite as I weighed it in my hands. Jack was very comfortable holding the weapon; his hands moved around it with practiced fluency. As he stared down the cracked barrel, he asked Derek:

"You guys 'pass shoot' here, right?"

"That's right. You won't find an Irishman in a punt among the reeds with a decoy. Ducks that respond to an Irish accent tend to make bad eating!"

Everyone else laughed knowingly, but I had no idea what they were talking about. Derek explained.

"You see Jack is the only one of you that is wearing camouflage? That's because in North America they hunt with decoys and duck calls, luring the birds in close so that they can fire at them—hence the camouflage. We don't have the patience for that. We shoot them as they fly past."

"It's a legacy of Vietnam," Jack said with a perfectly straight face. "All that hanging around the Mekong Delta in camouflage fatigues kind of got under our skin."

It was time to go. Though I had been in every make and model of four-wheel drive vehicle over the previous fifteen years, from Jeep to Porsche to Mercedes to BMW, I could not recall the last time I had been off-road in one. I smiled as I thought of the wax-polished, leather-interior SUVs that line the streets in Dublin's business district—many with low-profile tyres. We were a long way from that now, I thought, as my vertebrae cavorted like a concertina in a jig and my teeth came close to shattering. While I was being thrown around the front seat beside Derek, I caught a glimpse of

244

the other three, wedged shoulder to shoulder and immovable on the back seat—Henrik in the middle, Jack to his right, and Peter "the Beater" to his right. Peter, whose job it would be to flush out birds from the surrounding area and send them our way, was a great, corn-fed country lad with shoulders like a road bridge. Behind them, slavering and bobbing, were Jarvis and Joe, two panting cocker spaniels. Right now they were as excited and wound up as two teenagers on their way to their first rock festival, but in a few minutes they would be calm and still, obeying commands with robotic efficiency.

As Derek switched off the engine and we climbed out of the Jeep, the world changed. The grind and whine of the engine and suspension was replaced by the lapping of water and the whisper of wind in the trees, reeds, and grass. As I predicted, Jarvis and Joe had calmed down completely, their silent alertness accompanied by only the slightest rhythmic panting.

We followed Derek along the barely perceptible track that skirted the lake, while Peter the Beater disappeared into the foliage. Nobody spoke. As well as drinking in the atmosphere, we were under instructions from Derek to be as quiet as possible so as not to disturb the wild fowl we were hoping to shoot.

Finally, we took up our positions. In the agreed order, we took aim and fired at the birds as they passed. As my finger felt the cold chill of the trigger, I was very glad I had donned a pair of fingerless gloves. It was going to be a few long, cold hours.

Each shot gave a loud, echoing report across the landscape. It amazed me that any bird within a ten-mile radius would consider taking flight, but they did. For twenty minutes or so, succumbing to the charms of Peter the Beater, ducks would fly before us. I was surprised and relieved to find that I had a good eye and was able to hold my own. That being said, Jack was conducting his own massacre, hitting home with almost every shot.

Over the next few hours we changed location several times, with varying degrees of success in each place. At the end of the day, I was happy to be returning home with three plump mallard, one to be enjoyed now and the other two destined for the freezer.

As we tramped back through the crisp scrub grass and reeds towards where the Jeep was parked, I asked Jack how he had found pass shooting in comparison to sitting and waiting.

"I guess I kind of like the way you people do it here. I hate to sound like a broken record, but the way we hunt waterbirds at home is a bit like selling, and I don't know about you, but I like a break from the day job when I go outdoors.

"We put on our costumes and even a bit of make-up, then we get into a punt with a stack of decoys and a duck call. From then on, you're telling the ducks a story that isn't true. You want them to believe that the sound they're hearing is the sound of their buddies, that the bits of plastic floating in the water are also their buddies, and that you, all dressed up like a navy seal, are a tree. It's the kind of sales story you can only get away with telling if you're not interested in turning the prospect into a loyal customer. In the case of the ducks, I guess, it's a once only transaction.

"I'll be honest. I don't care whether you can play a duck call like John Coltrane—it's not for me. Our way is an ambush; your way is a hunt. You have the thrill of the chase and the level playing field of the open air."

It was working for him too. He had bagged more than anyone else. Henrik hadn't done badly, either. The day had been everything I had promised and everything he had wished for. Apparently, Irish wetlands compared very favourably to the Frisian Islands and the deltas of the North Sea. He had spent a great deal of time in deep conversation with Derek and Peter the Beater. I suspected he was looking into the idea of joining the club.

At this point, I had been in a great deal of places and situations with Jack because of the various ride-outs. It was strange, however, to be out here

246

in the open countryside with Henrik, whom I had only ever encountered in offices and function rooms. In the few weeks since we had last spoken of the subject, the RFP process had continued satisfactorily. I had helped Roger complete the official document, which had now been dispersed to my rivals. Working on the inside like this gave me an uncomfortable feeling, combining the guilt of subterfuge with a remote fear that it might not work. I was pondering this as we approached the Jeep and Henrik came up to me.

"Good work on the RFP. I've read it," he said conspiratorially.

"Thank you. That's good news," I replied.

"And Seb?" He was smiling as he held up his duck-laden sack.

"Don't worry about the contract. How do you say, 'It's in the bag!'"

Made in the USA
Charleston, SC
20 June 2014